AF868912

BUSINESS ISSUES, COMPETITION AND ENTREPRENEURSHIP

# SMALL BUSINESS TAX ISSUES AND BENEFITS

# BUSINESS ISSUES, COMPETITION AND ENTREPRENEURSHIP

Additional books in this series can be found on Nova's website at:

https://www.novapublishers.com/catalog/index.php?cPath=23_29&seriesp=Business+Issues%2C+Competition+and+Entrepreneurship

Additional e-books in this series can be found on Nova's website at:

https://www.novapublishers.com/catalog/index.php?cPath=23_29&seriespe=Business+Issues%2C+Competition+and+Entrepreneurship

BUSINESS ISSUES, COMPETITION AND ENTREPRENEURSHIP

# SMALL BUSINESS TAX ISSUES AND BENEFITS

ALTON E. KASTENBERG
EDITOR

**Nova Science Publishers, Inc.**
*New York*

Copyright © 2010 by Nova Science Publishers, Inc.

**All rights reserved.** No part of this book may be reproduced, stored in a retrieval system or transmitted in any form or by any means: electronic, electrostatic, magnetic, tape, mechanical photocopying, recording or otherwise without the written permission of the Publisher.

For permission to use material from this book please contact us:
Telephone 631-231-7269; Fax 631-231-8175
Web Site: http://www.novapublishers.com

**NOTICE TO THE READER**

The Publisher has taken reasonable care in the preparation of this book, but makes no expressed or implied warranty of any kind and assumes no responsibility for any errors or omissions. No liability is assumed for incidental or consequential damages in connection with or arising out of information contained in this book. The Publisher shall not be liable for any special, consequential, or exemplary damages resulting, in whole or in part, from the readers' use of, or reliance upon, this material. Any parts of this book based on government reports are so indicated and copyright is claimed for those parts to the extent applicable to compilations of such works.

Independent verification should be sought for any data, advice or recommendations contained in this book. In addition, no responsibility is assumed by the publisher for any injury and/or damage to persons or property arising from any methods, products, instructions, ideas or otherwise contained in this publication.

This publication is designed to provide accurate and authoritative information with regard to the subject matter covered herein. It is sold with the clear understanding that the Publisher is not engaged in rendering legal or any other professional services. If legal or any other expert assistance is required, the services of a competent person should be sought. FROM A DECLARATION OF PARTICIPANTS JOINTLY ADOPTED BY A COMMITTEE OF THE AMERICAN BAR ASSOCIATION AND A COMMITTEE OF PUBLISHERS.

**LIBRARY OF CONGRESS CATALOGING-IN-PUBLICATION DATA**

Small business tax issues and benefits / editor, Alton E. Kastenberg.
p. cm.
Includes index.
ISBN 978-1-61668-806-6 (hardcover)
1. Small business--Taxation--United States. I. Kastenberg, Alton E.
HJ2381.S54 2010
336.2'07--dc22

2010012277

*Published by Nova Science Publishers, Inc. ✢ New York*

# CONTENTS

# PREFACE

Federal, state and local taxes represent a major cost of doing business in the United States, and this is particularly true for small businesses. The array of federal taxes that small businesses face includes income taxes (individual and corporate), social security and Medicare employment taxes, excise taxes, and unemployment compensation taxes. This book explores the federal tax burden on small firms and its effects on their performance and rates of formation and growth.

Chapter 1 - Federal, state and local taxes represent a major cost of doing business in the United States, and this is particularly true for small businesses. The array of federal taxes that small businesses face includes income taxes (individual and corporate), social security and Medicare employment taxes, excise taxes, and unemployment compensation taxes.

Under the federal income tax system, a progressive statutory rate structure applies to income of businesses and individuals. The income of corporations is taxed twice, once at the corporate level through the payment of the corporate income tax, and again at the individual owner (level) of a corporation when corporate profits are distributed in the form of dividends or capital gains. Other forms of business, such as sole proprietorships, partnerships, S corporations, and limited liability companies, are not subject to an entity level tax, and business profits are taxed only at the individual owner level.

Calculating the overall costs of federal income taxes to small business owners requires an examination of both corporate and individual income taxes to explore who bears the burden of the taxes on business income. The federal income tax system is progressive, meaning that the tax rate increases as income increases and ranges from 10 percent to 35 percent under current law. In addition, exceptions to the normal tax rules (e.g., deductions, exclusions, and credits) can have the effect of lowering the overall tax rate actually imposed to a rate that is less than the statutory rate. Thus, there is a difference between the statutory tax rate imposed on business income and the effective tax rates that the small business (and its owners) may face. Effective tax rates provide a more accurate picture of how taxes are imposed on small business owners than statutory tax rates.

This research attempts to calculate the average effective tax rates faced by small businesses as a result of federal income taxes. The research explores how these effective tax rates vary depending upon the form of doing business (e.g., sole proprietorship, partnership, corporation, etc.), industrial classification, and business size. The research also examines the impact of special provisions in the federal tax laws that apply only to small businesses.

The primary methodological approach employed for purposes of this study is a microsimulation model in which aggregate (macro) outcomes are simulated "from the bottom up" by calculating tax liabilities at the entity level. This modeling framework is supported by use of the Public Use Statistics of Income (SOI) microdata file prepared annually by the Internal Revenue Service. The SOI data files are augmented with statistical imputations to trace the ultimate tax burden with respect to pass-through entities that do not pay federal income taxes directly.

The research detailed in this paper is limited to the effective tax rates imposed on small businesses by federal income taxes, due to the complexity of the analysis required for this study. This research could be extended to explore the effect of other federal taxes, such as federal estate taxes, excise taxes, employment taxes, and state and local government taxes to provide a better picture of the overall effect of taxes on small business in the United States.

Chapter 2 - Under the American Recovery and Reinvestment Act of 2009 (ARRA, P.L. 111-5), business taxpayers may expense (or deduct as a current expense) up to $250,000 of the total cost of certain depreciable assets placed in service in 2009, within certain limits. One limit is a phaseout threshold, which is set at $800,000 in 2009. The act also allows business taxpayers to claim a so- called bonus depreciation allowance in 2009 that is equal to 50% of the cost of qualified assets placed in service that year. Firms unable to use either option for accelerated depreciation have to write off that cost over a longer period, using current depreciation schedules. The rules governing the use of the allowance confine most of its benefits to relatively small firms.

This report focuses on the economic effects of what is referred to as the small business expensing allowance. It begins by explaining how the allowance works, then summarizes its legislative history and describes legislation in the 111th Congress to modify the allowance, and concludes with a discussion of the allowance's implications for economic efficiency, equity, and tax administration. The report will be updated as necessary.

There was strong bipartisan support for enhancing the expensing allowance in recent Congresses, and there are some early signs that this support has not waned in the 111th Congress. Several bills to extend the enhanced allowance that was in effect in 2008 through 2009 or 2010 have been introduced, capped by H.R. 1, the American Recovery and Reinvestment Act of 2009. The version of H.R. 1 signed by President Obama contains a provision that would allow firms to claim the same enhanced expensing allowance in 2009 that was available in 2008. The act also extends through 2009 the 50% bonus depreciation allowance that applied to the purchase of qualified assets in 2008.

The expensing allowance appears to have a minor effect on the composition and allocation of business investment, the distribution of the federal tax burden among income groups, and the cost of tax compliance for smaller firms. These effects correspond to the three traditional criteria for evaluating tax policy: efficiency, equity, and simplicity. While the allowance has the potential to spur increased small business investment by reducing the user cost of capital and increasing the cash flow of firms that use the allowance, it can also harm economic efficiency by encouraging greater investment in activities with relatively low pre-tax rates of return. At the same time, the allowance appears to have no measurable impact on the distribution of the federal tax burden among income groups, but it simplifies tax accounting for firms claiming it.

Provided certain conditions are met, firms may expense (or deduct as a current expense) up to $250,000 of the total cost of qualified assets they purchase and place in service in 2009. Some refer to this option for capital cost recovery as the small business expensing allowance, as the rules governing its use confine the allowance's benefits mainly to firms that are relatively small in asset, employment, or revenue size. Generally, firms that cannot use the expensing allowance may recover the cost of the same assets over longer periods by claiming allowable depreciation deductions. The expensing allowance represents a significant tax subsidy for small business investment, as it reduces the marginal effective rate at which the returns to investment in qualified assets are taxed.

The 111th Congress has already passed a bill (H.R. 1, the American Recovery and Reinvestment Act of 2009 or ARRA, P.L. 111-5) that extends through 2009 an enhanced version of the allowance that was available in 2008.

It is hoped that such an investment tax subsidy will spur many small firms to spend more on new equipment in 2009 than they otherwise would.

This report examines the current status of the small business expensing allowance, initiatives in the 111$^{th}$ Congress to modify it, and its main economic effects The report begins by describing the allowance's design and summarizing its legislative history. It then discusses proposals in the current Congress to modify the current allowance. The report concludes with an assessment of the allowance's implications for economic efficiency, equity, and tax administration.

Chapter 3 - The federal tax burden on small firms and its effects on their performance and rates of formation and growth is a policy issue that never seems to disappear from Congress's legislative agenda. Continuing congressional interest in the issue has led to the enactment of a series of legislative initiatives to reduce this burden in recent Congresses. In February 2009, the 111$^{th}$ Congress passed a bill (the American Recovery and Reinvestment Act of 2009, P.L. 111-5) intended to spur an economic recovery; it included several small business tax preferences.

This report describes the main federal tax benefits for small firms and examines the economic arguments for and against them. It will be updated as needed.

While a comprehensive estimate of the federal revenue cost of existing small business tax preferences cannot be made with available information, estimates by the Joint Committee on Taxation and the Treasury Department of the revenue lost because of the larger federal tax expenditures indicate that this cost will exceed $15 billion in FY2009. The following small business tax benefits appear to have the widest reach outside the agricultural sector: the taxation of small firms as passthrough entities; the graduated rate structure for the corporate income tax; the expensing allowance for equipment under Section 179 of the Internal Revenue Code; the exemption of some small corporations from the corporate alternative minimum tax; cash-basis accounting; a tax credit for costs incurred by small firms in establishing pension funds for employees; a tax credit for costs incurred by small firms in complying with the Americans with Disabilities Act; and the exclusion from taxation of capital gains on the sale or disposition of qualified small business stock.

These and other small business tax benefits raise some significant policy issues. For economists who specialize in public finance, a key issue is whether or not preferential tax treatment for small firms can be justified on economic grounds. If such a justification cannot be found, then proposals to extend or enhance small business tax preferences arguably could create more economic problems than they solve.

Proponents of granting tax relief to small firms say such relief is justified on several grounds. First, in their view, small firms create opportunities for social and economic advancement. Second, proponents maintain that the rate of small business formation responds favorably to reductions in tax burdens. Third, they note that small firms make important contributions to economic growth and employment over time. Fourth, small firms are thought to face special constraints on their ability to raise needed capital in debt and equity markets. Finally, proponents argue that tax preferences are needed to offset the financial burden placed on small firms as a result of complying with a variety of federal regulations.

Critics of small business tax preferences find it difficult to justify them on economic grounds. They say such preferences lessen the progressivity of the federal income tax and boost the returns on small business investment in ways that distort the domestic allocation of economic resources. In addition, critics contend that many existing small business tax preferences are inappropriate or poorly designed (or in some cases, both), magnifying any efficiency losses associated with them.

Some policy issues never seem to disappear from Congress's legislative agenda. One such issue is the federal tax burden on small firms and its effect on their formation, performance, and growth.

It appears that many lawmakers regard small firms in general as a vital and unsurpassed source of job creation, economic opportunity, and technological innovation. Many of these same individuals are also inclined to see current federal taxation of small firms both as an obstacle to their formation and a drag on their growth, and as an effective policy tool for boosting their rates of formation and growth. Recent Congresses have passed numerous laws that have included a variety of tax preferences for small firms. The 111$^{th}$ Congress has already proven to be no exception. In February 2009 it passed legislation (the American Recovery and Reinvestment Act of 2009, P.L. 111-5) to stimulate the economy that included several tax benefits targeted at small firms. Numerous other bills to extend or enhance existing small business tax benefits, or create new ones, have been introduced.

Existing small business tax benefits and proposals to enhance or expand them raise several policy issues. For most economists, a key policy issue is whether the benefits can be justified on economic grounds. If such a rationale cannot be found, or if the one set forth by proponents of small business tax benefits can be shown to rest on untenable assumptions, then critics of these benefits could be right in arguing that they damage social welfare in the long run. Another policy issue tied to small business tax benefits concerns the use of preferential tax treatment to extend assistance to small firms. The benefits entail costs in the guise of foregone tax revenues and the resources required on the part of the federal government to administer the tax benefits, and on the part of eligible small firms to comply with their requirements. Some question whether tax subsidies are more cost-effective than alternative approaches to providing assistance to small firms, such as grants, loan guarantees, and exemptions from certain federal regulations.

This report explores these issues by examining the main non-agricultural small business tax preferences and the economic arguments for and against them. It begins with a brief description of existing preferences for small firms, then reviews what is known about the economic contributions of small firms, and concludes with a discussion of the principal economic arguments for and against these subsidies.

In: Small Business Tax Issues and Benefits ISBN: 978-1-61668-806-6
Editors: Alton E. Kastenberg © 2010 Nova Science Publishers, Inc.

*Chapter 1*

# EFFECTIVE FEDERAL INCOME TAX RATES FACED BY SMALL BUSINESSES IN THE UNITED STATES

***SBA, Office of Advocacy***

## INTRODUCTION

Federal, state and local taxes represent a major cost of doing business in the United States, and this is particularly true for small businesses. The array of federal taxes that small businesses face includes income taxes (individual and corporate), social security and Medicare employment taxes, excise taxes, and unemployment compensation taxes.

Under the federal income tax system, a progressive statutory rate structure applies to income of businesses and individuals. The income of corporations is taxed twice, once at the corporate level through the payment of the corporate income tax, and again at the individual owner (level) of a corporation when corporate profits are distributed in the form of dividends or capital gains. Other forms of business, such as sole proprietorships, partnerships, S corporations, and limited liability companies, are not subject to an entity level tax, and business profits are taxed only at the individual owner level.

Calculating the overall costs of federal income taxes to small business owners requires an examination of both corporate and individual income taxes to explore who bears the burden of the taxes on business income. The federal income tax system is progressive, meaning that the tax rate increases as income increases and ranges from 10 percent to 35 percent under current law. In addition, exceptions to the normal tax rules (e.g., deductions, exclusions, and credits) can have the effect of lowering the overall tax rate actually imposed to a rate that is less than the statutory rate. Thus, there is a difference between the statutory tax rate imposed on business income and the effective tax rates that the small business (and its owners) may face. Effective tax rates provide a more accurate picture of how taxes are imposed on small business owners than statutory tax rates.

This research attempts to calculate the average effective tax rates faced by small businesses as a result of federal income taxes. The research explores how these effective tax rates vary depending upon the form of doing business (e.g., sole proprietorship, partnership, corporation, etc.), industrial classification, and business size. The research also examines the impact of special provisions in the federal tax laws that apply only to small businesses.

The primary methodological approach employed for purposes of this study is a microsimulation model in which aggregate (macro) outcomes are simulated "from the bottom up" by calculating tax liabilities at the entity level. This modeling framework is supported by use of the Public Use Statistics of Income (SOI) microdata file prepared annually by the Internal Revenue Service. The SOI data files are augmented with statistical imputations to trace the ultimate tax burden with respect to pass-through entities that do not pay federal income taxes directly.

The research detailed in this paper is limited to the effective tax rates imposed on small businesses by federal income taxes, due to the complexity of the analysis required for this study. This research could be extended to explore the effect of other federal taxes, such as federal estate taxes, excise taxes, employment taxes, and state and local government taxes to provide a better picture of the overall effect of taxes on small business in the United States.

# I. Executive Summary

This study provides a comprehensive look at the effects of the federal income tax system on small businesses in the United States.[1] This is accomplished by combining data contained on federal income tax returns of corporations and individuals and utilizing an integrated methodological framework that allows for a comparison of the effects of these taxes across different taxpayer groups.

The study explores the effective tax rates imposed by the federal income tax system on small businesses organized as sole proprietorships, partnerships, limited liability companies (LLCs), S corporations, and C corporations. For this purpose, the study uses the following data sources from the IRS Statistics of Income Public Use Files:

For sole proprietorships, Form 1040, Schedule C (individual income tax return, schedule of profit and loss from business);

For partnerships, LLCs, and S corporations, Form 1040, Schedule E (individual income tax return, schedule of supplemental income and loss); and

For C corporations, Form 1120 (corporation income tax return).

For classification purposes, the IRS defines small businesses as those entities with less than $10 million of assets. For consistency, we use a modified threshold of $10 million in gross receipts. Under this threshold, 26.8 million of the total 28.7 million business income tax returns filed in 2004 constituted nonfarm small business returns. Thus, for 2004, small business returns represented more than 93 percent of all business tax returns. Of these 26.8 million returns, 19.2 million were sole proprietorships, 2.3 million were partnerships (including LLCs), 3.3 million were S corporations, and 2.0 million were C corporations.

More than 50 percent of small businesses filing federal income tax returns in 2004 had gross receipts of less than $25,000. More than 83.9 percent of the small businesses making less than $25,000 were sole proprietorships. In fact, nonfarm sole proprietorships with gross receipts of less than $25,000 represented 48.7 percent of all U.S. small businesses in 2004. Almost 88 percent of all small business tax returns filed in 2004 had gross receipts of no more than $250,000.

Measuring the effect of federal income taxes on business income presents a complex task that can be approached in a variety of ways. While many people think of the statutory tax rate when they consider the effect of federal income taxes, the reality is that the statutory tax rate does not represent the best measure of the effect of taxes on a business. Instead, a better measure examines the effective tax rates that businesses face. There are two general measures of effective tax rates – average effective tax rates and marginal effective tax rates. Average effective tax rates provide a measure of the overall effect of taxes on business income, whereas marginal effective tax rates generally measure the effect of taxes on a specific investment. This paper examines average effective tax rates.

An effective tax rate is usually calculated as the amount of tax paid by the firm as a fraction of net income or profit. Generally, the effective tax rate paid by a business will differ from the statutory rate because of the effect of the graduated rate structure and the deductions or credits that are allowed. Effective tax rates can also be affected because the statutory incidence of a tax may not reflect who ultimately bears the burden of the tax.

Average effective tax rates can provide a useful measure of whether firms in similar circumstances pay similar levels of tax. More likely, though, when otherwise similar firms face markedly different effective tax rates, it usually suggests that one firm is utilizing special provisions in the tax law – provisions that may or not be available to other firms – that can serve to reduce taxes. Thus, average effective tax rates can theoretically offer a measure of how the form of doing business, such as a corporation or sole proprietorship, affects the overall federal income tax burden. In addition, average effective tax rates can be used to examine the effects of federal income taxes in other ways, such as whether one industry faces more or less tax than another industry or how business size affects average effective tax rates.

Small businesses in the United States pay an estimated average effective tax rate of approximately 19.8 percent.[2] The analysis in this study found that, of the entities subject to federal income tax at the business owner level, small business sole proprietorships face the lowest average effective tax rate at 13.3 percent. Small business partnerships face an average effective tax rate of 23.6 percent, and small business S corporations face an average effective tax rate of 26.9 percent. These calculations include only those entities with positive net income for the 2004 tax year.

Small business C corporations, on the other hand, face an average effective tax rate of 17.5 percent. However, the calculations for C corporations are conceptually different than those for other entity types and, thus, are not directly comparable. First, due to data constraints, the effective tax rate calculations for C corporations do not capture the salaries paid by C corporations to their owners. Because salaries paid to C corporation owners will generally be deductible by the C corporation (to the extent they constitute reasonable compensation for services), the effective tax rate of the corporation can be reduced by these payments, but the federal income tax payments by C corporation owners on these salary amounts are not captured in the calculations.[3] On the other hand, income received by owners of sole proprietorships and pass-through entities generally is not deductible and is reflected in the effective tax rate calculation.

Second, the profits of C corporations are distributed to shareholders in the form of dividends and capital gains that are taxable to the individual owner. However, the existing data do not allow the tracing of C corporation dividend payments to specific owners for the purpose of calculating the effective tax rate attributable to these corporate distributions.

Some of the variation in effective tax rates by entity type can be traced to the legal form of organization of the businesses. For example, nearly 60 percent of all small business sole proprietorships have net income of less than $10,000 and an average effective tax rate of 8.1 percent and only 3.1 percent have net income of at least $100,000. On the other hand, 30.8 percent of S corporations have net income less than $10,000 and more than 18 percent have net income of at least $100,000.

Variations in effective tax rates can also occur depending upon the industry in which the business is conducted. Some of these variations will occur because of the differences in the way the businesses are conducted. For example, a manufacturing business will likely generate bigger business deductions than a service industry business. In addition, there are a variety of special tax provisions applicable to small businesses for federal income tax purposes.[4] These provisions often provide a special tax benefit for small businesses in a specific industry. For the affected taxpayers, these provisions can have a significant effect on effective tax rates. However, because the scope of these provisions is often quite narrow, their overall impact on the average effective tax rates of small businesses will likely be quite small. Because the Individual Income Tax Public Use File does not provide industry specific data, this study imputes the industry of the taxpayer to provide a suggestion of how effective tax rates may vary by industry group (see Section VII for more detail).

## II. Overview

Federal income taxes represent some of the most significant costs of doing business for most U.S. companies. In addition to these direct costs – measured by the amount of tax liability that is owed – taxes can impose indirect costs as well by altering business decisions that firms may make. These business decisions can be fundamental to the operation of the company: deciding whether to invest in new equipment, hiring new employees, and the choice of organizational structure. Small businesses often face competitive disadvantages in U.S. and world markets because they lack the economies of scale that large businesses have, and they have less access to the capital markets. Small businesses may face an additional disadvantage to the extent that the federal tax system affects small businesses differently than large businesses.

In the United States, the federal income tax is imposed on the taxable income of corporations, individuals, and trusts. Taxable income is a business' gross income minus business deductions. The federal income tax is progressive, meaning that the statutory rate of tax increases as taxable income increases.

Very little is known about the true effect of federal taxes on small businesses because the data necessary to calculate these effects is difficult to obtain in a consistent and reliable manner. In addition, because the form of doing business affects the overall federal income taxes paid, and because small businesses interact with the federal tax system in a variety of other ways (such as through the payroll tax system), the overall tax burden that small businesses face is often not transparent.

As a first step in tackling this problem, this study provides a comprehensive look at the effects of the federal income tax system on small businesses in the United States.[5] This is accomplished by combining data contained on federal income tax returns of corporations and individuals and utilizing an integrated methodological framework that allows for a comparison of the effects of these taxes across different taxpayer groups. We believe that this is the first empirical study of this type.

Measuring the effect of federal income taxes on business income presents a complex task that can be approached in a variety of ways. While many people think of the statutory tax rate when they consider the effect of federal income taxes, the reality is that the statutory tax rate does not represent the best measure of the effect of taxes on a business. Instead, a better measure examines the effective tax rates that businesses face. There are two general measures of effective tax rates – average effective tax rates and marginal effective tax rates. Average effective tax rates provide a measure of the overall effect of taxes on business income, whereas marginal effective tax rates generally measure the effect of taxes on a specific investment. In this paper, we examine average effective tax rates.

Effective tax rates faced by businesses are usually interpreted as the actual tax rates paid by firms. An effective tax rate is usually calculated as the amount of tax paid by the firm as a fraction of income or profit. Generally, the effective tax rate paid by a business will differ from the statutory rate because of the effect of the graduated rate structure and the deductions or credits that are allowed. Effective tax rates can also be affected because the statutory incidence of a tax may not reflect who ultimately bears the burden of the tax.

Average effective tax rates can provide a useful measure of whether firms in similar circumstances pay approximately the same level of tax. More likely, though, when otherwise similar firms face markedly different effective tax rates, it usually suggests that one firm is utilizing special provisions in the tax law – which may not be available to other firms – to reduce taxes. Thus, average effective tax rates can theoretically offer a measure of how the form of business, such as a corporation or sole proprietorship, affects the overall federal income tax burden. In addition, average effective tax rates can be used to examine the effects of federal income taxes in other ways, such as whether a particular industry faces greater or lesser federal income taxes relative to another industry or how business size affects average effective tax rates.

However, calculating the effective tax rate paid by small businesses in the United States can be difficult and imprecise for a variety of reasons. First, the effective tax rate will be calculated differently depending upon the form of business. There are five common organizational structures that a small business may choose – a C corporation, an S corporation, a partnership, a limited liability company, and a sole proprietorship. For federal income tax purposes, a C corporation is subject to two levels of federal income tax – the C corporation pays tax directly on its taxable income, and the owners of the corporation are also subject to federal income tax on the business gains that they receive in the form of dividends and capital gains. All other forms of small businesses are called "pass through" entities and are not subject to an entity-level federal income tax; instead, the income of the business is passed through to the owners of the business and taxed on their individual income tax returns. Most limited liability companies are treated as partnerships for federal income tax purposes; a very small fraction of these entities are treated as sole proprietorships.

For purposes of calculating effective tax rates, in the case of a corporation, the effective tax rate should take into account not only the federal income taxes paid directly by the corporation, but also the federal individual income taxes paid on corporate dividends distributed to shareholders and the income taxes paid by the individual owners of corporate equities when they realize their capital gains.[6]

Measuring effective tax rates can also be difficult because there are a variety of deductions, exclusions, and credits that potentially affect the effective tax rate paid by small businesses.

Some of these provisions are specifically intended for small businesses, whereas other provisions are available to all businesses irrespective of size. Cataloguing the numerous federal income tax provisions that may affect a business's effective tax rate and calculating the extent to which such provisions are utilized is a challenging task.

Finally, some small businesses may be involved in multinational operations, which presents unique problems because the business may be eligible for foreign tax credits. These credits will affect the U.S. federal effective tax rate and may distort the business' overall effective tax rate if the taxes paid to foreign governments are not considered. However, the vast majority of multinational business operations are conducted by large corporations and attempting to consider the effects of these operations with respect to U.S. small businesses is outside the scope of this research.

This study relies on information from several publicly available sources to calculate the effective federal income tax rate faced by small businesses by tracing income to its eventual, taxable destination. In addition, the study examines what provisions in the tax law are most effective in helping small businesses reduce their taxes.

Microsimulation is utilized as the primary methodological approach in calculating effective tax rates. In microsimulation, aggregate tax liabilities are calculated "from the bottom up," by calculating the individual tax liabilities of the constituent economic units and summing these units to arrive at an economy-wide total. To calculate these effective rates, publicly available, micro-level data on individual taxpayers is utilized together with a sophisticated software program that allows the calculation of these rates separately for the basic taxpayer entity types.

In the case of small businesses that are not subject to an entity-level tax, the pass-through nature of the small business income is explored to calculate the actual tax rates faced by the owners of the businesses. This is accomplished by examining publicly available tax return information that identifies income from partnerships and S corporations separately. The tax return data also provides information that permits the calculation of effective tax rates incurred by sole proprietorships. For small businesses that are organized as corporations (other than S corporations), detailed tabulations of corporate income, deductions and taxes made available by the Internal Revenue Service (IRS) are utilized.

The following sections provide an overview of small businesses in the United States (Section III), review the relevant literature to date on the tax burden facing small businesses (Section IV), provide an overview of the federal income tax system and its impact on small businesses and their owners (Section V), summarize the methodological approach to measuring effective tax rates of small businesses (Section VI), and present the principal findings of the research across various taxpayer groups delineated by entity type, size, and industry (Section VII). Appendix A provides a technical description of the methodology utilized in the study, and Appendix B contains a list of special provisions of the federal income tax law system that are applicable to small businesses.

## III. Small Businesses in the United States

Small businesses constitute an essential element of the U.S. economy. Approximately 30 million small businesses operate in the United States, making up the vast majority of employer firms in the country. Collectively, these small businesses employ nearly 80 million workers or approximately half of all private sector employees.

A balanced mix of large and small businesses contributes to the health of the U.S. economy. While large businesses can achieve economies of scale, have broader reach, and are better able to diversify risks, small businesses benefit from greater flexibility, fewer bureaucratic controls, and the ability to provide unique products and services to niche markets. Some industries tend to be dominated by small businesses, while others are more likely to be dominated by large businesses.

### Identifying Small Businesses

The standard of what constitutes a small business for data collection purposes varies depending upon the use of the data. For example, there are different definitions of small businesses for federal contracting purposes and federal tax purposes. There is no uniform and consistent definition; rather, different definitions may be based on the (1) number of employees, (2) business receipts, or (3) business assets.

For research purposes, the SBA Office of Advocacy often defines a small business as an independent business that has fewer than 500 employees. Other, more specific, small business size standards have been developed by the SBA for federal contracting purposes. These standards are based on business receipts, number of employees, or total assets. For example, many types of farming use a threshold of $750,000 of gross receipts to define a small business. Many manufacturing businesses have a size standard of less than 500 employees. Some financial institutions, like commercial banks, have an asset threshold ($175 million).

Special small business provisions also apply for federal tax purposes.[7] These provisions typically apply based either on gross receipts or number of employees. In addition, some federal tax provisions, such as the provision that permits a limited dollar amount of equipment purchases to be expensed, rather than depreciated, have the effect of providing a benefit to small businesses because of the way in which they are typically structured.

For classification purposes, the IRS generally considers a business small if it has total assets of less than $10 million. The standard used in this study is less than $10 million in gross receipts.

## Data on Small Businesses in the United States[8]

Federal income tax returns filed by businesses provides a wealth of information about businesses operating in the United States. Some of this information is presented below. In order to assure the confidentiality of information contained on administrative tax returns, however, data items in the Public Use File are rounded and often masked or blurred to prevent identification. As such, each individual tax record is only suggestive of an actual tax return filed.

Business organization can take several forms – the choice of business form affects both the application of the federal income tax system as well as the application of state laws relating to the liability of business owners. Among the possible business forms that can be used are the following:

**Sole Proprietorships.** A sole proprietorship is a business that has one owner and does not have stock.

**Partnerships.** A partnership is a group of entities (e.g., individuals or businesses) that organize to do business together. Each partner contributes money, property, labor, or skill and shares in the profits of the business.

**C Corporations.** C corporations are formed when prospective shareholders exchange money, property, or both in exchange for capital stock of the corporation. The return on a shareholder's investment in a C corporation is paid either through dividends or through the capital gains that are realized when the shareholder sells his or her stock in the corporation.[9]

**S Corporations.** S corporations are small business corporations that are afforded the benefits of limited liability like C corporations, but can elect to be treated as a pass- through entity for federal income tax purposes.

**Limited Liability Company (LLC).** Limited liability companies are relatively new business structures that are authorized under state law. Owners of an LLC, like a corporation, have limited personal liability, but other features of an LLC function more like a partnership, such as the flow-through treatment of LLC owner income. Most LLCs are treated as partnerships for federal tax purposes, although a very small percentage of LLCs are treated as sole proprietorships.[10] Some separate information concerning LLCs is provided in this section. However, for purposes of the effective tax rate calculations later in this study, LLCs are included in either the sole proprietorship or partnership calculations based on whether they file as a sole proprietorship or partnership for federal income tax purposes.

The most prevalent form of business in the United States is the sole proprietorship. In 2004, 20.6 million nonfarm sole proprietorships filed with the IRS, compared to 2.0 million C corporations, 3.5 million S corporations, and 2.5 million partnerships (including returns of LLCs) for a total of 28.7 million nonfarm business returns filed.

Using the threshold of $10 million in gross receipts, 26.8 million of the 28.7 million returns filed in 2004 constituted nonfarm small businesses; these returns represented more than 93 percent of all business tax returns. Table 1 shows the breakdown of small businesses in the Unites States by entity type for 2004.

**Table 1. Number of Small Businesses by Entity Type, 2004**

| Entity Type | Number |
|---|---|
| C Corporation | 2.0 million |
| S Corporation | 3.3 million |
| Partnership (including LLCs) | 2.3 million |
| Nonfarm Sole Proprietorship | 19.2 million |
| Total Nonfarm Small Businesses | 26.8 million |

Source: IRS Statistics of Income

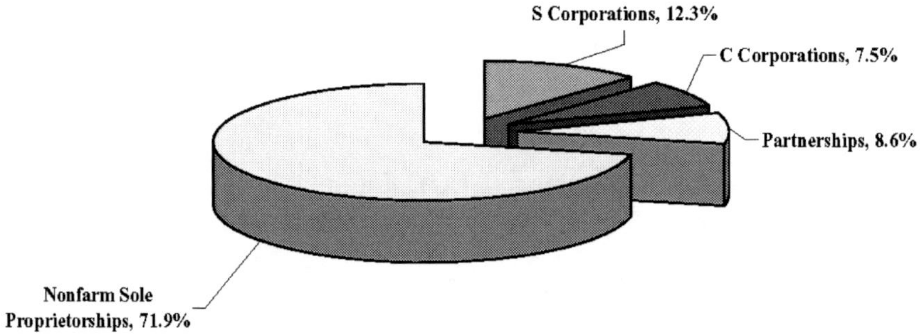


Source: IRS Statistics of Income

Graph 1. Distribution of Small Business Entities by Type, 2004

Graph 1 shows the percentage distribution of small businesses by entity type for 2004. Sole proprietorships account for 71.7 percent of all small businesses in the United States. While some sole proprietors can have sufficient numbers of employees or gross receipts to qualify as a large business, most sole proprietorships in the United States (19.2 million of the total 20.6 million sole proprietorships or 93.2 percent) are small businesses.

## Growth of Businesses by Entity Type over Time

Since 1995, the number of business tax returns filed by C corporations and farms has declined. On the other hand, there has been significant growth in the number of sole proprietorships, limited liability companies, and S corporations filing business tax returns. Table 2 shows the changes in the number of businesses in the United States by entity type since 1995.

**Table 2. Number of Businesses by Entity Type, 1995-2005 (in thousands)**

| Year | Sole Props[1] | C Corps | S Corps | Partnerships[2] | LLCs[3] | Farms | Total |
|---|---|---|---|---|---|---|---|
| 1995 | 16,424 | 2,321 | 2,153 | 1,462 | 119 | 2,219 | 24,698 |
| 1996 | 16,955 | 2,327 | 2,304 | 1,433 | 221 | 2,188 | 25,429 |
| 1997 | 17,176 | 2,258 | 2,452 | 1,410 | 349 | 2,161 | 25,806 |
| 1998 | 17,398 | 2,261 | 2,588 | 1,359 | 496 | 2,092 | 26,194 |
| 1999 | 17,576 | 2,210 | 2,726 | 1,306 | 631 | 2,068 | 26,516 |
| 2000 | 17,903 | 2,185 | 2,860 | 1,287 | 771 | 2,087 | 27,092 |
| 2001 | 18,338 | 2,149 | 2,986 | 1,254 | 878 | 2,007 | 27,613 |
| 2002 | 18,926 | 2,112 | 3,154 | 1,208 | 1,034 | 1,995 | 28,429 |
| 2003 | 19,710 | 2,060 | 3,342 | 1,283 | 1,092 | 1,997 | 29,484 |
| 2004 | 20,591 | 2,040 | 3,518 | 1,188 | 1,359 | 2,005 | 30,700 |
| 2005 | 21,468 | 1,987 | 3,684 | 1,199 | 1,565 | 1,981 | 31,884 |

[1] Some sole proprietorship returns represent single member LLCs and these returns are included in the totals for sole proprietorships. For the years 2001-2005, there were the following numbers of sole proprietorships registered as LLCs: 126,437 (2001), 146,839 (2002), 220,615 (2003), 309,665 (2004), and 455,734 (2005).

[2] Does not include LLCs filing partnership returns.

[3] Prior to 1998, domestic limited liability partnerships were not separately identified on the partnership return. Thus, the total number of LLCs is understated for 1995-1997.

Source: IRS Statistics of Income.

Table 2 shows that, from the period 1995 to 2005, the total number of business income tax returns increased by 29.1 percent from 24.7 million to 31.9 million. The majority of the increase (5 million) represents increases in the number of sole proprietorships. In addition, LLCs and S corporations showed significant increases, from 119,000 to 1.6 million in the case of LLCs and from 2.2 million to 3.7 million in the case of S corporations. These increases are primarily attributable to changes in the law that made these forms of organization more attractive. The growth in LLCs can be attributed to changes in state laws that allowed the formation of limited liability companies and modifications to federal law to allow these entities to operate as pass-through entities like partnerships for federal income tax purposes. The increase in the number of S corporation returns is partly attributable to changes in the law that increased the number of S corporation shareholders and otherwise made it easier for corporations to qualify for S corporation status.

During the same 1995 to 2005 period, the number of C corporations declined from 2.3 million to 1.99 million, the number of returns of partnerships that were not LLCs declined from 1.5 million to 1.2 million, and the number of farm returns declined from 2.2 million to 1.98 million.

Graph 2 shows the changes in the number of business entities by business form from 1995 to 2005, for selected years. As the graph demonstrates, the upward trend in business income tax returns is substantially attributable to the increase in sole proprietorships.

## Small Business Gross Receipts Data

While sole proprietorships are the dominant form of business in the United States, most sole proprietorships are very small. IRS data for 2004 shows the distribution of business entities by gross receipts (see Table 3). Of the 15.9 million small business returns with receipts less than $25,000, 13.3 million (84 percent) were sole proprietorships. In fact, nonfarm sole proprietorships with gross receipts of less than $25,000 represented 48.7 percent of all U.S. small businesses in 2004.

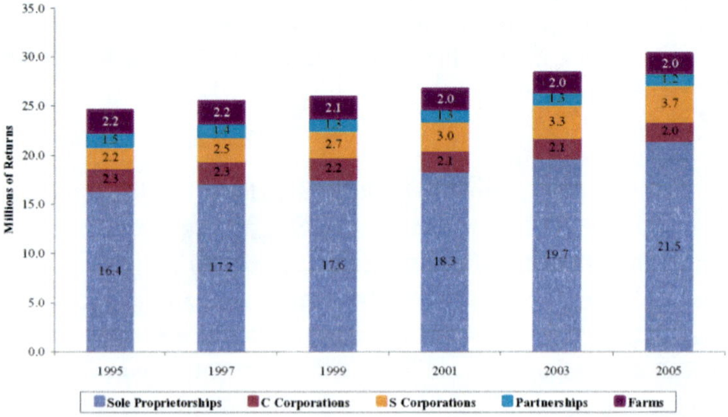


Source: IRS Statistics of Income

Graph 2. Changes in Types of Business Income Tax Returns (Selected Years, 1995-2005)

**Table 3. Number of Small Businesses by Size of Business Receipts and Entity Type, 2004**

| Size of Gross Business Receipts | All Small Businesses | Corporations | | Non-Corporate Businesses | |
|---|---|---|---|---|---|
| | | C Corp | S Corp | Partnerships | Nonfarm Sole Proprietorships |
| Less than $25,000 | 15,872,235 | 450,597 | 829,112 | 1,284,396 | 13,308,130 |
| $25,001 to $100,000 | 5,521,119 | 307,399 | 561,043 | 397,461 | 4,255,216 |
| $100,001 to $250,000 | 2,578,962 | 328,012 | 601,851 | 262,423 | 1,386,675 |
| $250,001 to $500,000 | 1,331,692 | 268,188 | 451,424 | 147,948 | 464,131 |
| $500,001 to $1 million | 932,913 | 247,385 | 375,165 | 110,698 | 199,666 |
| $1,000,001 to $2.5 million | 686,257 | 229,634 | 291,775 | 89,675 | 75,173 |
| $2,500,001 to $5 million | 263,212 | 103,484 | 107,685 | 36,829 | 15,213 |
| $5,000,001 to $10 million | 143,693 | 57,788 | 60,895 | 20,925 | 4,085 |
| Total | 27,330,082 | 1,987,171 | 3,684,086 | 2,350,355 | 19,708,289 |

Source: IRS Statistics of Income.

Table 3 shows that about 58 percent of small businesses filing federal income tax returns in 2004 had gross receipts of less than $25,000. Almost 88 percent of all small business tax returns filed in 2004 had gross receipts of no more than $250,000. By contrast, only one-half of one percent of small businesses had gross receipts of more than $5 million in 2004, and only 2.8 percent of these entities were sole proprietorships.

Another interesting aspect of these figures is that, for the smallest size class, the percentage of small businesses by entity type declines from sole proprietorship to partnership to S corporation to C corporation. The reverse is also true; C corporations and S corporations constitute a larger percentage of small businesses with gross receipts between $5 million and $10 million, while sole proprietorships constitute a small percentage of these businesses. Graph 3, below, shows that C corporations constitute 2.8 percent of small businesses with gross receipts under $25,000, while they constitute 40.2 percent of small businesses with gross receipts between $5 million and $10 million. Sole proprietorships constitute 83.9 percent of small businesses with gross receipts of less than $25,000 and only 2.8 percent of small businesses with gross receipts between $5 million and $10 million. Sole proprietorships become a consistently smaller percentage of small businesses as the gross receipts class increases and C corporations and S corporations become a consistently larger percentage of the total.

A somewhat different picture emerges by examining the net income of small businesses. Table 4 shows the net income of small businesses in 2004 (excluding those with losses) by size of gross receipts and entity type.

There is far less concentration of net income across size classes and entity types. For example, while the smallest size class (less than $25,000 of gross receipts) represents about 58 percent of all small businesses; these businesses earn slightly less than 15 percent of net income. Likewise, in the largest size class ($5,000,001 – $10 million of gross receipts), the representative share of net income is 20 times the share of total small businesses. Across all size classes, the distribution of net income is much more uniform, with most size classes earning between 10 percent and 12 percent of total small business net income. More than half of small business income is earned by businesses organized either as partnerships or S corporations. This suggests that there may be benefits to a more complicated organization structure as the business grows. Interestingly, C corporations accrue only about 8 percent of total small business net income.

The distribution of small businesses varies significantly by industry. Some industries are better suited to the small business model, while other industries are better supported by larger more complex business structures. This occurs for a variety of reasons. For example, a larger business will have easier access to capital, which will be important to businesses in industries with large investments in plant and equipment. Similarly, an industry that benefits from having multiple locations may be better suited to a larger business structure. Table 5 summarizes information on the number of small businesses by entity type and industry.

The largest concentration of small businesses is in the services industry (with 3.7 million in professional, scientific, technical and management services and 9.2 million in other services), which accounts for almost half of all small businesses.

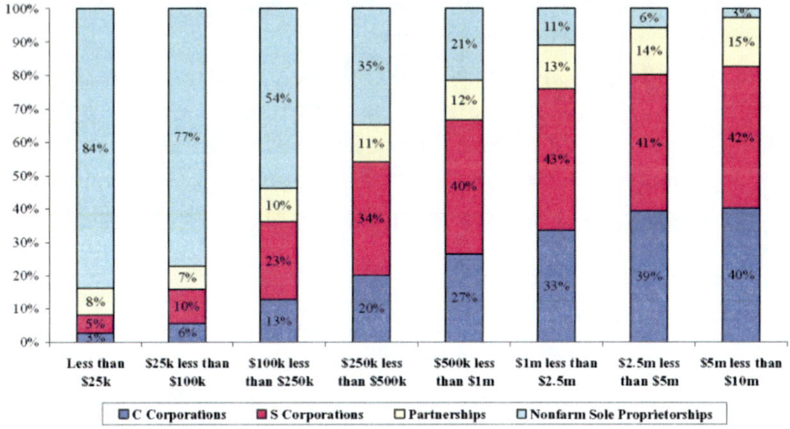


Source: IRS Statistics of Income

Graph 3. Percentage Distribution of Business Firm Type by Gross Receipts, 2004

**Table 4. Net Income of Small Businesses by Size of Business Receipts and Entity Type, 2004 ($million)**

| Size of Gross Business Receipts | All Small Businesses | Corporations | | Non-Corporate Businesses | |
|---|---|---|---|---|---|
| | | C Corps | S Corps | Partnerships | Nonfarm Sole Propri-etorships |
| Less than $25,000 | $101,958 | $6,895 | $23,682 | $29,381 | $41,999 |
| $25,001 to $100,000 | 102,216 | 2,196 | 7,578 | 13,033 | 79,410 |
| $100,001 to $250,000 | 102,435 | 3,450 | 14,633 | 19,941 | 64,410 |
| $250,001 to $500,000 | 76,935 | 3,543 | 17,698 | 18,303 | 37,391 |
| $500,001 to $1 million | 76,558 | 5,547 | 23,107 | 22,320 | 25,585 |
| $1,000,001 to $2.5 million | 86,431 | 9,620 | 33,836 | 29,996 | 12,979 |
| $2,500,001 to $5 million | 66,104 | 10,148 | 26,296 | 26,001 | 3,660 |
| $5,000,001 to $10 million | 70,947 | 15,771 | 22,184 | 31,070 | 1,923 |
| **Total** | **$683,585** | **$57,169** | **$169,015** | **$190,045** | **$267,356** |

Source: IRS Statistics of Income

The service sector is generally more localized and better suited to the small business model. After services, the next largest concentrations of small businesses are in finance, insurance and real estate; wholesale and retail trade; and construction. No discernible trend appears to exist with respect to how companies are organized across industries; however, a somewhat larger fraction of companies in the agriculture, construction, and manufacturing sectors are organized as C corporations than might be expected by their numbers.

**Table 5. Number of Small Businesses by Industry Classification and Entity Type, 2004**

| Industry Classification (NAICS) | All Small Businesses | Corporations | | Non-Corporate Businesses | |
|---|---|---|---|---|---|
| | | C Corps | S Corps | Partnerships | Nonfarm Sole Propri-etorships |
| Agriculture, Fore-stry, Fishing and Hunting | 527,397 | 61,279 | 80,422 | 121,508 | 264,188 |
| Mining | 184,169 | 13,000 | 16,292 | 27,547 | 127,331 |
| Utilities | 19,774 | 5,308 | 2,908 | 2,029 | 9,528 |
| Construction | 3,289,119 | 221,581 | 438,968 | 137,485 | 2,491,084 |
| Manufacturing | 606,155 | 119,169 | 140,363 | 37,591 | 309,031 |
| Wholesale and Retail Trade | 3,793,927 | 385,271 | 538,693 | 165,985 | 2,703,978 |
| Transportation and Warehousing | 1,152,417 | 77,427 | 101,077 | 29,320 | 944,594 |
| Information | 414,601 | 51,178 | 65,733 | 30,788 | 266,901 |
| Finance, Insurance & Real Estate | 3,869,232 | 296,322 | 505,291 | 1,335,016 | 1,732,603 |
| Professional, Sci-entific, Technical | 3,720,574 | 265,667 | 531,765 | 170,370 | 2,752,772 |
| Other Services | 9,223,338 | 493,420 | 854,831 | 290,449 | 7,584,638 |
| **Total, All Industries** | 26,800,703 | 1,989,62 | 3,276,342 | 2,348,088 | 19,186,649 |

**Table 6. Employment Size of Establishments, 2005 and 2006**

| Employment Size of Establishment | Number of Establishments | | Number of Employees | | Annual payroll ($million) | |
|---|---|---|---|---|---|---|
| | 2005 | 2006 | 2005 | 2006 | 2005 | 2006 |
| All establishments | 7,499,702 | 7,601,160 | 116,317,003 | 119,917,165 | $4,482,722 | $4,792,43 |
| 1 to 4 employees | 4,119,363 | 4,137,018 | 6,880,381 | 6,932,206 | 272,716 | 286,987 |
| 5 to 9 employees | 1,411,199 | 1,432,352 | 9,351,264 | 9,502,160 | 290,053 | 303,848 |
| 10 to 19 employees | 937,617 | 964,024 | 12,642,173 | 12,994,803 | 407,124 | 429,877 |
| 20 to 49 employees | 636,625 | 658,710 | 19,229,836 | 19,872,543 | 644,851 | 687,476 |
| 50 to 99 employees | 219,324 | 227,125 | 15,072,272 | 15,631,618 | 532,558 | 572,096 |
| 100 to 249 employees | 125,027 | 130,048 | 18,716,560 | 19,444,384 | 713,468 | 767,941 |
| 250 to 499 employees | 31,834 | 32,704 | 10,874,791 | 11,171,950 | 462,769 | 495,646 |
| 500 to 999 employees | 11,845 | 12,121 | 8,052,708 | 8,247,601 | 375,531 | 400,745 |
| 1,000 employees or more | 6,868 | 7,058 | 15,497,018 | 16,119,900 | 783,653 | 847,812 |

Source: U.S. Department of Commerce, Bureau of the Census: County Business Patterns, 2005 and 2006.

Note: An establishment is a single physical location of a business. A single firm may have one or more establishments. The data include all operating establishments with one or more paid employees. The series excludes data on self-employed individuals, employees of private households, railroad employees, agricultural production employees, and most government employees.

## Small Businesses by Employment Levels

While this study defines small businesses solely by reference to total receipts (i.e., total annual gross receipts of less than $10 million), another way of looking at small businesses is by looking at employment size. Census survey data for 2005 and 2006 provide information on business size, total employment, and annual payroll, which is summarized in Table 6. This data includes businesses with at least one paid employee, but excludes self-employed individuals with no paid employees, employees of private households, railroad employees, agricultural production workers, and most government employees.

The data show that there are approximately 7.5 million establishments with employees in the United States. Table 7 shows the percentage distribution of establishments in the United States for 2006, by establishment size. Nearly 90 percent of all establishments have fewer than 20 employees. Furthermore, 99.75 percent of all establishments have fewer than 500 employees. Of the approximately 120 million private sector employees in the United States in 2006, 80 percent worked for an establishment with fewer than 500 employees.

In addition to the data concerning establishments by employment size, there are also a large number of U.S. businesses that are referred to as nonemployer entities; most of these entities are sole proprietorships. For 2006, approximately 21 million U.S. businesses did not have employees. These businesses had more than $970 billion of receipts. Table 8 shows the number of establishments in the United States without employees for 2006 by business form.

Statistics of Income data from the IRS enable a closer look at the specific types of business forms to glean additional information about businesses in the United States.

## Sole Proprietorships

For 2004, there were approximately 19.7 million individual income tax returns for nonfarm sole proprietorships in the United States, and 19.2 million of these returns were small businesses.[11] Graph 4 shows that 68 percent of the sole proprietorship returns filed in 2004 had gross receipts of less than $25,000, and nearly 90 percent of these returns had gross receipts of less than $100,000. The data confirm the commonly held view that sole proprietors are significantly more likely to be small businesses than other types of business entities.

Businesses in certain industries are more likely to be conducted through sole proprietorships. Businesses in the professional, scientific, and technical services industry (15 percent), construction (13 percent), retail trade (12 percent), and other services (11 percent) industries comprise over 50 percent of all businesses filing sole proprietorship returns. Table 9 summarizes 2004 sole proprietor return data by industry sector and shows the number of returns, total business receipts, total business deductions, and profits.

Sole proprietorships in some industries are more profitable than those in other industries. Among the more profitable industries, sole proprietorships in the professional, scientific, and technical services industry represented 15 percent of total returns, but had 23 percent of net income. Similarly, sole proprietorships in the real estate and rental and leasing industry had 6 percent of total returns and 12 percent of net income. Sole proprietorships in the finance and insurance industry made up 3 percent of all sole proprietorship returns, but these businesses had 7 percent of total sole proprietorship net income. On the other hand, sole proprietorships in the retail trade industry represent 12 percent of all sole proprietorship returns, but these businesses had only 3 percent of all sole proprietorship net income.

Average receipts for all sole proprietorships for 2004 were $56,416, average deductions equaled $44,080, and average net income equaled $12,357.

**Table 7. Distribution of Establishments by Size, 2006**

| Employment Size of Establishment | Number of Establishments | Share of Total | Cumulative Share |
|---|---|---|---|
| 1 to 4 employees | 4,137,018 | 54.4% | 54.4% |
| 5 to 9 employees | 1,432,352 | 18.8% | 73.3% |
| 10 to 19 employees | 964,024 | 12.7% | 85.9% |
| 20 to 49 employees | 658,710 | 8.7% | 94.6% |
| 50 to 99 employees | 227,125 | 3.0% | 97.6% |
| 100 to 249 employees | 130,048 | 1.7% | 99.3% |
| 250 to 499 employees | 32,704 | 0.4% | 99.8% |
| 500 to 999 employees | 12,121 | 0.2% | 99.9% |
| 1,000 employees or more | 7,058 | 0.1% | 100.00% |
| All establishments | 7,601,160 | 100.00% | 100.00% |

Source: U.S. Department of Commerce, Bureau of the Census: County Business Patterns, 2006.

**Table 8. Nonemployer Businesses in the United States, 2006**

| Entity Form | Number of Entities | Receipts ($million) |
|---|---|---|
| All establishments | 20,768,555 | $970,384 |
| Corporations | 1,353,461 | 166,145 |
| Sole proprietorships | 18,177,466 | 632,027 |
| Partnerships | 1,237,628 | 172,212 |

Source: IRS Statistics of Income.

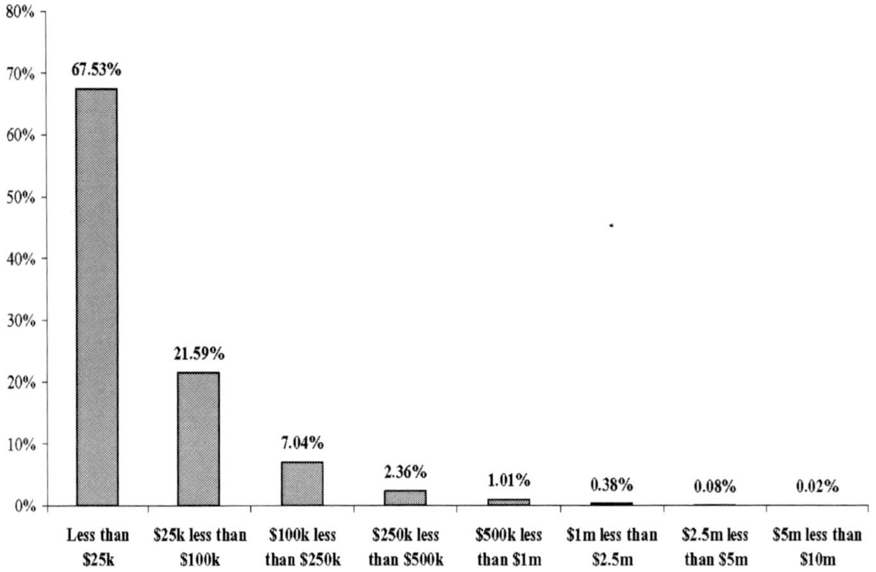


Source: IRS Statistics of Income

Graph 4. Percentage Distribution of Sole Proprietorships, by Gross Receipts, 2004

Graph 5, below, shows the 2004 business receipts for sole proprietorships for selected industry sectors. Businesses in three sectors – the construction; retail trade; and professional, scientific, and technical services fields – make up nearly 50 percent of all sole proprietorship receipts.

Data from the IRS provide information on the sources of business expenses for sole proprietorships. In 2004, sole proprietorships claimed a total of $892.4 billion of deductions on individual income tax returns. Of these deductions, $521 billion represented business expense deductions.

**Table 9. Sole Proprietor Returns by Industry Sector, 2004**

| Industry Sector | Number of Returns (thousands) | Percent of Total | Total Business Receipts ($million) | Percent of Total | Total Business Deductions ($million) | Percent of Total | Profits ($million) | Percent of Total |
|---|---|---|---|---|---|---|---|---|
| **All nonfarm industries** | 19,621 | 100% | $1,106,934 | 100% | $864,885 | 100% | $242,449 | 100% |
| Construction | 2,587 | 13% | 198,364 | 18% | 167,343 | 19% | 31,038 | 13% |
| Manufacturing | 351 | 2% | 25,825 | 2% | 22,901 | 3% | 3,018 | 1% |
| Wholesale trade (merchant wholesalers) | 351 | 2% | 40,850 | 4% | 35,735 | 4% | 5,129 | 2% |
| Retail trade | 2,399 | 12% | 187,077 | 17% | 179,018 | 21% | 8,102 | 3% |
| Transportation and warehousing | 983 | 5% | 65,304 | 6% | 56,584 | 7% | 8,756 | 4% |
| Information | 295 | 2% | 8,044 | 1% | 6,141 | 1% | 1,902 | 1% |
| Finance and insurance | 673 | 3% | 73,126 | 7% | 55,556 | 6% | 17,599 | 7% |
| Real estate and rental and leasing | 1,179 | 6% | 70,504 | 6% | 42,592 | 5% | 27,907 | 12% |
| Professional, scientific, and technical services | 2,951 | 15% | 137,682 | 12% | 80,934 | 9% | 56,862 | 23% |
| Administrative and support and waste management | 1,995 | 10% | 49,987 | 5% | 35,936 | 4% | 14,075 | 6% |
| Educational services | 474 | 2% | 6,926 | 1% | 4,471 | 1% | 2,456 | 1% |
| Health care and social assistance | 1,778 | 9% | 104,159 | 9% | 62,205 | 7% | 41,963 | 17% |
| Arts, entertainment, and recreation | 1,132 | 6% | 26,359 | 2% | 20,572 | 2% | 5,793 | 2% |
| Accommodation & food services | 384 | 2% | 39,721 | 4% | 38,338 | 4% | 1,391 | 1% |
| Other services | 2,089 | 11% | 73,006 | 7% | 56,560 | 7% | 16,458 | 7% |

Source: IRS Statistics of Income.

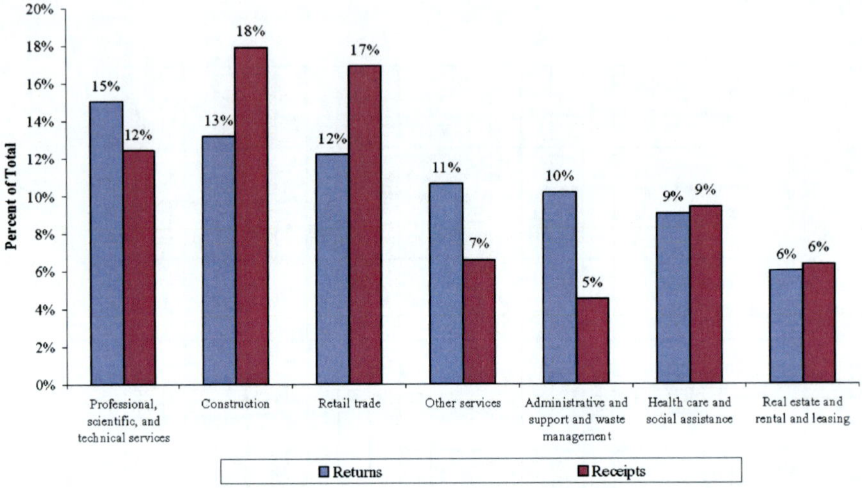


Source: IRS Statistics of Income

Graph 5. Sole Proprietorship Returns and Receipts, as a Percentage of Totals, Selected Industries, 2004

Graph 6 ranks the top business expense deductions claimed by sole proprietorships in 2004 for federal income tax purposes. Graph 6 shows that salaries and wages ($71.1 billion for 2004) were the top business expense deduction for sole proprietorships, accounting for 13.5 percent of all sole proprietor business expense deductions, while car and truck expenses ($59.0 billion) accounted for 11 percent of the total.[12] Depreciation deductions, which include amounts eligible for expensing under section 179 of the Internal Revenue Code, totaled $42.9 billion in 2004.

## Partnerships and Limited Liability Companies (LLCs)

Partnerships are unincorporated businesses organized by two or more persons (or entities, such as corporations) to carry on a trade or business. Each partner contributes money, property, skill, or labor to the partnership, and the partners share profits and expenses.

The following four primary types of entities are treated as partnerships for federal income tax purposes: (1) domestic general partnerships, (2) domestic limited partnerships, (3) domestic limited liability companies, and (4) domestic limited liability partnerships. There are a relatively small number of foreign partnerships and entities classified as other partnerships for data purposes. Table 11 summarizes the number of partnerships by type and by the net income or loss. Several years have been selected to show the change in the types of entities filing as partnerships over time.

**Table 10. Components of Nonfarm Sole Proprietorship Business Deductions, 2004***

| Deduction Category | Total Amount ($million) | Average Amount |
|---|---|---|
| **Total Deductions** | $892,402 | $43,340 |
| Cost of Sales and Operations | 370,951 | 18,015 |
| Advertising expenses | 12,888 | 626 |
| Car and truck expenses | 58,980 | 2,864 |
| Commissions | 13,267 | 644 |
| Contract labor | 24,687 | 1,199 |
| Depletion | 776 | 38 |
| Depreciation | 42,901 | 2,084 |
| Employee benefit programs | 2,618 | 127 |
| Insurance | 18,864 | 916 |
| Legal and professional services | 8,959 | 435 |
| Meals and entertainment deducted | 5,998 | 291 |
| Mortgage interest | 5,167 | 251 |
| Other interest paid on business indebtedness | 5,856 | 284 |
| Office expenses | 12,363 | 600 |
| Pension and profit-sharing plans | 1,202 | 58 |
| Rent on machinery and equipment | 8,728 | 424 |
| Rent on other business property | 28,139 | 1,367 |
| Repairs | 14,762 | 717 |
| Supplies | 27,303 | 1,326 |
| Salaries and wages | 71,069 | 3,451 |
| Taxes paid | 16,036 | 779 |
| Travel | 10,318 | 501 |
| Utilities | 21,477 | 1,043 |
| Other business deductions | 98,293 | 4,774 |
| Home office business deductions | 7,807 | 379 |

Source: IRS Statistics of Income.

* Details in the table do not add to total deductions because the costs of sales and operations have been excluded from the table above. The costs of sales and operations include such items as inventory (beginning and end of year), cost of labor, purchases, and material supplies.

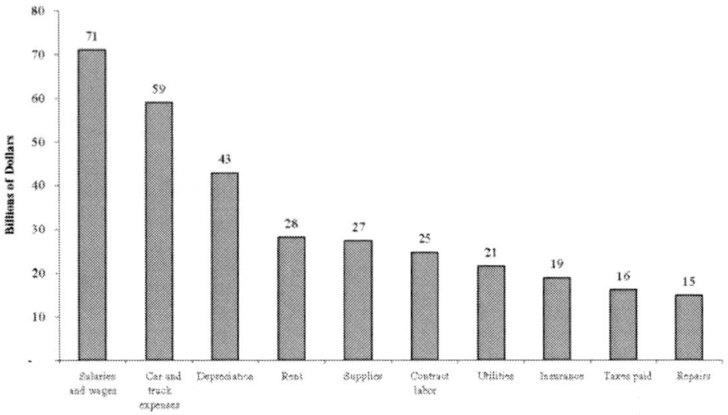


Source: IRS Statistics of Income

Graph 6. Top Deductions Claimed by Sole Proprietorships, 2004

## Table 11. Number of Partnerships, by Type of Entity and Profit Status, Selected Years (Number of partnerships in thousands)

| | 1995 | 2000 | 2004 | 2005 | Percent Change, 1995-2005 |
|---|---|---|---|---|---|
| **Total Number of Partnerships**[1] | 1,581 | 2,058 | 2,547 | 2,764 | 74.8% |
| **Domestic General Partnerships** | 1,167 | 872 | 725 | 729 | -37.5% |
| Net Income | 739 | 589 | 474 | 486 | -34.2% |
| Loss | 428 | 283 | 251 | 243 | -43.2% |
| **Domestic Limited Partnerships** | 295 | 349 | 403 | 414 | 40.3% |
| Net Income | 157 | 215 | 245 | 255 | 62.4% |
| Loss | 138 | 134 | 158 | 159 | 15.2% |
| **Domestic Limited Liability Companies** | 119 | 720 | 1,270 | 1,465 | 1,131.1% |
| Net Income | 60 | 385 | 632 | 746 | 1,143.3% |
| Loss | 59 | 335 | 638 | 719 | 1,118.6% |
| **Domestic Limited Liability Partnerships** | n/a | 53 | 89 | 100 | n/a |
| Net Income | n/a | 32 | 53 | 60 | n/a |
| Loss | n/a | 21 | 36 | 40 | n/a |

Source: IRS Statistics of Income.

[1] Summary data on foreign partnerships and other partnerships are excluded from the table. Therefore, the total number of partnerships exceeds the sum of the data in this table.

n/a = These types of partnerships were not separately identified on the partnership return, but their numbers are included in the total partnership returns.

**Table 12. Partnerships, Returns by Industry Sector, 2004**

| Industry Sector | Number of Returns (thousands) | Percent of Total | Total Business Receipts ($million) | Percent of Total | Total Business Deductions ($million) | Percent of Total | Profit ($million) | Percent of Total |
|---|---|---|---|---|---|---|---|---|
| All nonfarm partnerships | 2,547 | 100% | $2,571,776 | 100% | $2,568,528 | 100% | $183,158 | 100% |
| Construction | 155 | 7% | 226,165 | 9% | 213,472 | 8% | 18,351 | 10% |
| Manufacturing | 43 | 2% | 616,213 | 24% | 595,370 | 23% | 33,033 | 18% |
| Wholesale trade | 43 | 2% | 357,070 | 14% | 352,250 | 14% | 9,763 | 5% |
| Retail trade | 136 | 6% | 281,853 | 11% | 286,785 | 11% | 1,550 | 1% |
| Transportation and warehousing | 34 | 1% | 71,204 | 3% | 70,996 | 3% | 4,689 | 3% |
| Information | 35 | 1% | 178,121 | 7% | 186,105 | 7% | 1,639 | 1% |
| Finance and insurance | 269 | 11% | 149,980 | 6% | 199,869 | 8% | 32,741 | 18% |
| Real estate and rental and leasing | 1,180 | 50% | 117,900 | 5% | 131,581 | 5% | 9,254 | 5% |
| Professional, scientific, and technical services | 164 | 7% | 231,711 | 9% | 189,299 | 7% | 54,159 | 30% |
| Administrative and support services | 52 | 2% | 52,851 | 2% | 51,439 | 2% | 3,158 | 2% |
| Education services | 8 | 0% | 3,084 | 0% | 3,003 | 0% | 148 | 0% |
| Health care and social assistance | 57 | 2% | 119,105 | 5% | 110,459 | 4% | 15,685 | 9% |
| Arts, entertainment, and recreation | 45 | 2% | 34,543 | 1% | 40,871 | 2% | (1,450) | -1% |
| Accommodation and food services | 91 | 4% | 114,480 | 4% | 119,556 | 5% | (104) | 0% |
| Other services | 58 | 2% | 17,497 | 1% | 17,471 | 1% | 541 | 0% |

Source: IRS Statistics of Income.

Note: Details may not add to total due to rounding.

Compared to the 21.5 million sole proprietorships in the United States in 2005, there were only 2.8 million partnerships (including LLCs). The data show that the growth in the total number of partnership returns is substantially related to the growth in the number of limited liability companies. From 1995 to 2005, the total number of limited liability companies grew more than 1,000 percent, from 119,000 returns in 1995 to 1.5 million returns in 2005. This growth is primarily attributable to changes in state and federal laws in the 1 990s that permitted the formation of limited liability companies, allowing business owners the limited liability protection of a corporation without the burden of corporate income tax.

Partnerships tend to be more prevalent in certain industries. Table 12 shows the percentage of all domestic partnerships, percentage of total business receipts, percentage of business deductions, and percentage of net income of domestic partnerships by industry sector. This data includes domestic general partnerships and domestic limited partnerships. While partnerships in the finance and insurance sector account for approximately 11 percent of all domestic partnerships, they have 18 percent of the net income of all domestic partnerships. Real estate and rental and leasing partnerships account for 50 percent of all partnerships but only about 5 percent of the net income of such partnerships. Partnerships in the manufacturing sector account for only about 2 percent of all domestic partnerships, but have about 18 percent of the net income.

Table 13 provides an overview of the sources of partnership business deductions in 2004.

Compared to sole proprietorships, with average deductions per entity of $44,000, partnerships have average total deductions of $1.1 million. This suggests that partnerships tend to be much larger entities than sole proprietorships. The top three business deductions for partnerships were salaries and wages, depreciation, and interest paid.

## S Corporations

There were approximately 3.4 million S corporation tax returns filed in the United States during tax year 2004. Approximately 98 percent of these returns reported receipts under $10 million and could be classified as small businesses.[13]

**Table 13. Components of Partnership Business Deductions, 2004**

| Deduction Category | Total Amount ($million) | Average Amount |
|---|---|---|
| **Total Deductions** | **$2,815,181** | **$1,105,346** |
| Cost of goods sold | 1,666,146 | 654,192 |
| Salaries and wages | 268,807 | 105,544 |
| Guaranteed payments to partners | 32,213 | 12,648 |
| Rent paid | 50,403 | 19,790 |
| Interest paid | 64,457 | 25,308 |
| Taxes and licenses | 42,114 | 16,536 |
| Bad debts | 12,771 | 5,014 |
| Repairs and maintenance | 15,515 | 6,092 |
| Depreciation | 90,231 | 35,428 |
| Depletion | 695 | 273 |
| Retirement plans, etc. | 7,947 | 3,120 |
| Employee benefit programs | 19,178 | 7,530 |
| Net loss from other partnerships and fiduciaries | 26,003 | 10,210 |
| Farm net loss | 3,792 | 1,489 |
| Net loss, noncapital assets | 2,201 | 864 |
| Other deductions | 512,706 | 201,308 |

Table 14 provides additional details on S corporation returns by industry sector, including the number of returns, business receipts and deductions, and net income for each sector. Wholesale and retail trade comprised 18 percent of all S corporation returns filed in 2004. The professional, scientific, and technical services sector followed closely with 16 percent and the construction sector with 14 percent of S corporation returns. Real estate and rental leasing sector filed the next largest share with 12 percent of all returns.

As shown in Table 14, the percentage of total returns and percentage of total receipts displayed a consistent relationship across all S corporation sectors. However, there were a few noteworthy discrepancies. (Graph 7 shows S corporation receipts and returns as a percentage of total receipts and returns for selected industry sector.)

Wholesale and retail trade, while filing the greatest percentage of returns (18 percent), reported significantly more receipts with 43 percent of all S corporation receipts. Construction had 14 percent of returns and 15 of receipts. However, the professional, scientific, and technical services sector reported 16 percent of all returns and only 6 percent of receipts.

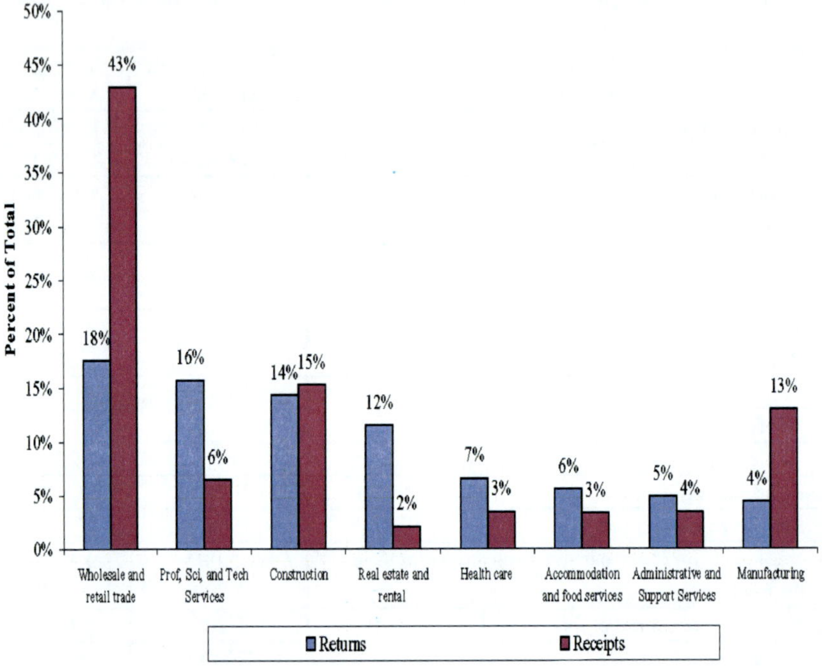


Source: IRS Statistics of Income

Graph 7. S Corporations Returns and Receipts, as a Percentage of Totals, for Selected Industry Sectors, 2004

The business deductions reported by S corporations varied from those reported by sole proprietors and partnerships. The average amount of deductions for sole proprietorships was approximately $43,000 for 2004; the average for partnerships was $650,000; and the average for S corporations was $830,000. Overall, S corporations reported that the cost of goods sold was by far the largest business deduction, accounting for approximately 65 percent of total deductions. Compensation of officers and salaries and wages was a distant second; they comprised collectively about 15 percent of total deductions. Table 15 presents the total and average business deductions claimed by S corporations, and Graph 8 displays the top 10 deductions claimed by S corporations (other than cost of goods sold).

The remaining business deductions claimed by S corporations were smaller than those claimed for cost of goods sold and officers' and employee compensation.

## Table 14. S Corporation Nonfarm Returns, by Industry Sector, 2004

| Industry Sector | Number of Returns (thousands) | Percent of Total | Total Business Receipts ($million) | Percent of Total | Total Business Deductions ($million) | Percent of Total | Profit ($million) | Percent of Total |
|---|---|---|---|---|---|---|---|---|
| **All Nonfarm Industries** | 3,418 | 100% | $4,553,288 | 100% | $4,426,553 | 100% | $273,464 | 100% |
| Construction | 489 | 14% | 696,960 | 15% | 673,273 | 15% | 38,916 | 14% |
| Manufacturing | 151 | 4% | 591,729 | 13% | 567,207 | 13% | 37,332 | 14% |
| Wholesale and retail trade | 599 | 18% | 1,956,730 | 43% | 1,932,252 | 44% | 58,074 | 21% |
| Transportation and warehousing | 107 | 3% | 138,167 | 3% | 136,528 | 3% | 6,196 | 2% |
| Information | 71 | 2% | 63,489 | 1% | 61,260 | 1% | 8,284 | 3% |
| Finance and insurance | 142 | 4% | 97,111 | 2% | 94,416 | 2% | 19,611 | 7% |
| Real estate and rental and leasing | 395 | 12% | 97,638 | 2% | 93,711 | 2% | 14,542 | 5% |
| Professional, scientific, and technical services | 538 | 16% | 295,285 | 6% | 273,105 | 6% | 33,220 | 12% |
| Holding companies | 25 | 1% | 6,697 | 0% | 12,722 | 0% | 6,717 | 2% |
| Administrative and support services | 168 | 5% | 159,368 | 4% | 153,743 | 3% | 10,685 | 4% |
| Education services | 28 | 1% | 12,781 | 0% | 11,617 | 0% | 1,510 | 1% |
| Health care and social assistance | 226 | 7% | 158,958 | 3% | 143,890 | 3% | 19,656 | 7% |
| Arts, entertainment, and recreation | 83 | 2% | 37,112 | 1% | 36,024 | 1% | 4,942 | 2% |
| Accommodation and food services | 192 | 6% | 153,186 | 3% | 150,802 | 3% | 8,728 | 3% |
| Other services | 204 | 6% | 88,077 | 2% | 86,003 | 2% | 5,052 | 2% |

Source: IRS Statistics of Income.

## C Corporations

There were approximately 2 million C corporation tax returns filed in the United States for the 2004 tax year. Approximately 97 percent of these filers reported receipts under $10 million and could be classified as small businesses. Graph 9 shows the share of small C corporations as a percentage of all C corporations. It is important to note the dramatic difference between large and small C corporations. While the vast majority of C corporation returns were filed by small businesses, these small C corporations accounted for only 16 percent of total receipts. Consequently, using aggregate data provides more relevant information for large C corporations.

Table 16 provides additional details on C corporation returns by industry sector, showing the number of returns, business receipts and deductions, and net income for each sector. The largest concentration of C corporations were found in wholesale and retail trade (19 percent); professional, scientific, and technical services (16 percent); and construction (15 percent). The real estate (8 percent), health care (8 percent), and manufacturing (5 percent) sectors followed closely behind.

**Table 15. Components of S Corporation Business Deductions, 2004**

| Deduction Category | Total Amount ($million) | Average Amount |
|---|---|---|
| **Total deductions (all industries)** | $4,518,457 | $1,284,260 |
| Cost of goods sold | 2,916,564 | 828,962 |
| Compensation of officers | 173,784 | 49,394 |
| Salaries and wages | 490,131 | 139,308 |
| Repairs | 28,546 | 8,114 |
| Bad debts | 9,654 | 2,744 |
| Rent paid on business property | 117,669 | 33,444 |
| Taxes paid | 100,563 | 28,583 |
| Interest paid | 39,141 | 11,125 |
| Amortization | 6,338 | 1,801 |
| Depreciation | 86,589 | 24,611 |
| Depletion | 504 | 143 |
| Advertising | 43,880 | 12,472 |
| Pension, profit-sharing, stock, annuity | 19,034 | 5,410 |
| Employee benefit programs | 42,819 | 12,170 |
| Net loss, noncapital assets | 1,021 | 290 |
| Other deductions | 442,221 | 125,691 |

Source: IRS Statistics of Income.

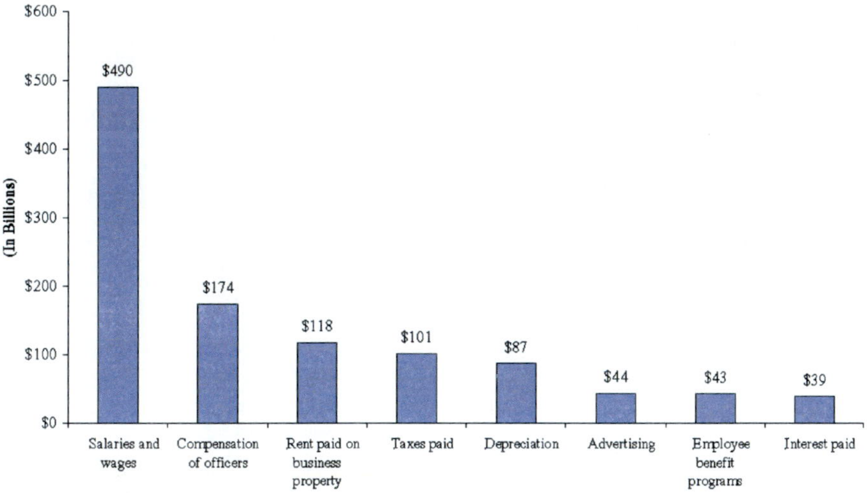


Source: IRS Statistics of Income

Graph 8. Top Deductions Claimed by S Corporations, 2004

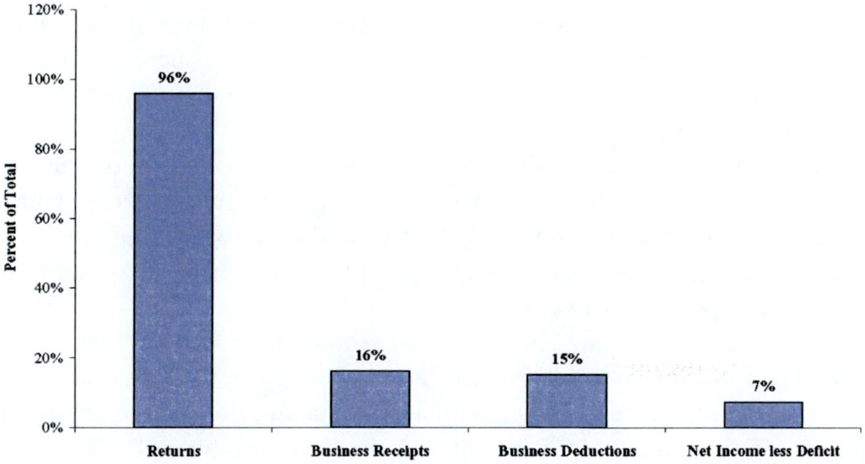


Source: IRS Statistics of Income

Graph 9. Small C Corporations as a Percentage of All C Corporations, 2004

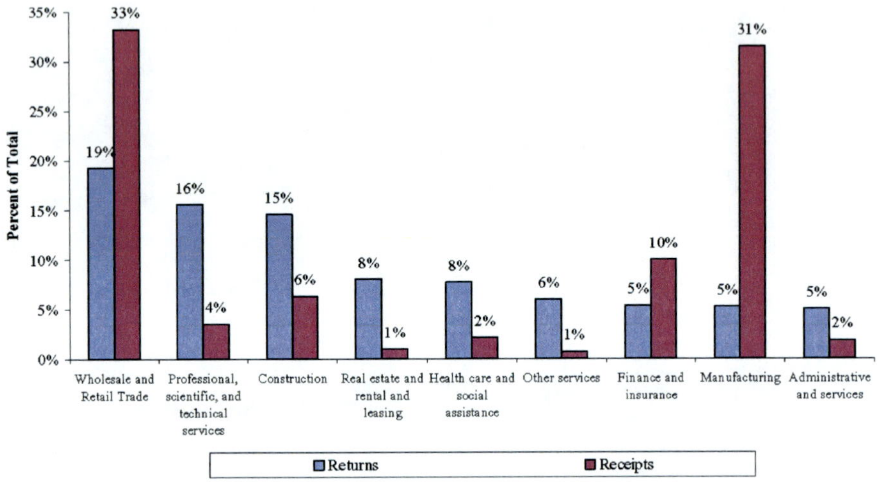


Source: IRS Statistics of Income

Graph 10. C Corporations Returns and Receipts, as a Percentage of Totals, for Selected Industry Sectors, 2004

Just as with S corporations, certain sectors of C corporations have an inverse relationship between returns and receipts. For instance, manufacturing reported only 5 percent of returns, but comprised 31 percent of all C corporation receipts. Refer to Graph 10 for C corporation returns and receipts distributed by industry sector.

While wholesale and retail trade comprised 19 percent of all returns, they reported 33 percent of all receipts. Conversely, the construction sector, with 15 percent of all returns, reported only 6 percent of total receipts. Similarly, the finance and insurance sector comprised only 5 percent of all returns but reported a 10 percent share of receipts.

The business deductions reported by C corporations were similar to those reported by S corporations. Overall, the cost of goods sold was the largest business deduction for C corporations, accounting for approximately 63 percent of their total deductions. Similarly, compensation of officers and salaries and wages comprised collectively about 12 percent of total deductions as the next largest category of business deduction. However, unlike some of the other business types, one other category of business deduction – interest paid – was prominent for C corporations, comprising 5 percent of the total deductions.[14]

## Table 16. C Corporation Returns by Industry Sector, 2004

| Industry Sector | Number of Returns (thousands) | Percent of Total | Total Business Receipts ($million) | Percent of Total | Total Business Deductions ($million) | Percent of Total | Profit ($million) | Percent of Total |
|---|---|---|---|---|---|---|---|---|
| **All Nonfarm Industries** | 3,021 | 100% | $15,277,194 | 100% | $16,288,207 | 100% | $1,405,868 | 100% |
| Construction | 440 | 15% | 967,136 | 6% | 924,628 | 6% | 61,976 | 4% |
| Manufacturing | 157 | 5% | 4,804,013 | 31% | 4,881,779 | 30% | 367,100 | 26% |
| Wholesale and retail trade | 584 | 19% | 5,077,236 | 33% | 5,003,864 | 31% | 196,670 | 14% |
| Transportation and warehousing | 100 | 3% | 383,775 | 3% | 377,002 | 2% | 21,742 | 2% |
| Information | 59 | 2% | 590,366 | 4% | 619,287 | 4% | 75,717 | 5% |
| Finance and insurance | 161 | 5% | 1,527,842 | 10% | 2,194,371 | 13% | 395,631 | 28% |
| Real estate and rental and leasing | 243 | 8% | 151,837 | 1% | 147,651 | 1% | 27,734 | 2% |
| Professional, scientific, and technical services | 472 | 16% | 537,193 | 4% | 507,021 | 3% | 52,202 | 4% |
| Management of holding companies | 19 | 1% | 168,670 | 1% | 594,217 | 4% | 121,893 | 9% |
| Administrative and services | 150 | 5% | 282,964 | 2% | 275,809 | 2% | 18,432 | 1% |
| Educational services | 25 | 1% | 25,946 | 0% | 23,645 | 0% | 3,088 | 0% |
| Health care and social assistance | 232 | 8% | 325,953 | 2% | 306,847 | 2% | 29,172 | 2% |
| Arts, entertainment, and recreation | 56 | 2% | 46,053 | 0% | 44,404 | 0% | 6,480 | 0% |
| Accommodation and food services | 143 | 5% | 277,147 | 2% | 281,412 | 2% | 20,442 | 1% |
| Other services | 180 | 6% | 111,065 | 1% | 106,269 | 1% | 7,589 | 1% |

Source: IRS Statistics of Income.

**Table 17. Components of C Corporation Business Deductions, 2004**

| Deduction Category | Total Amount ($million) | Average Amount |
|---|---|---|
| **Total Deductions (all industries)** | $16,861,357 | $5,410,406 |
| Cost of goods sold | 9,959,047 | 3,195,620 |
| Compensation of officers | 306,107 | 98,223 |
| Salaries and wages | 1,656,350 | 531,483 |
| Repairs | 100,145 | 32,134 |
| Bad debts | 99,739 | 32,004 |
| Rent paid on business property | 293,747 | 94,256 |
| Taxes paid | 345,525 | 110,871 |
| Interest paid | 767,652 | 246,321 |
| Charitable contributions | 11,443 | 3,672 |
| Amortization | 94,319 | 30,265 |
| Depreciation | 473,305 | 151,872 |
| Depletion | 9,592 | 3,078 |
| Advertising | 190,175 | 61,023 |
| Pension, profit-sharing, stock, annuity | 122,278 | 39,236 |
| Employee benefit programs | 227,170 | 72,893 |
| Net loss, noncapital assets | 14,241 | 4,570 |
| Other deductions | 2,190,520 | 702,886 |

Source: IRS Statistics of Income.

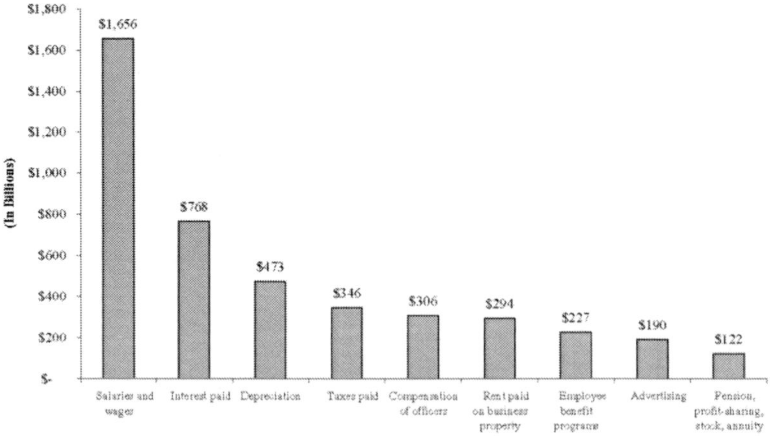


Source: IRS Statistics of Income

Graph 11. Top Deducations Claimed by C Corporations, 2004

The business deductions claimed by C corporations were relatively smaller for the remaining business deduction categories. Table 17 presents the total and average business deductions claimed by C corporations and Graph 11 displays the top 10 deductions claimed by C corporations.

## IV. Literature Review

Effective tax rates are a useful way to summarize the federal income tax burden of both small and large businesses. Effective tax rates provide a benchmark from which to evaluate one aspect of tax equity: a tax system can be deemed fair if similarly situated firms pay roughly the same rate of tax. When there are large differences in the tax rates paid by different taxpayer segments, this may suggest that inequities or asymmetries exist in the tax system. Quite often, special provisions in the tax law give rise to these differences. These special provisions may not be available to or utilized effectively by all taxpayers.

Researchers have studied the impact of federal income taxes on businesses in the United States for many years. Most studies look at large multinational corporations; very few studies have specifically considered small businesses in a comprehensive manner. There are several reasons for this. First, there are conceptual hurdles to overcome relating to who bears the ultimate burden of the tax. Second, there are difficult measurement issues to consider in tracing out the tax payments of the business. And third, the data necessary to compute accurate measures of effective tax rates are not collected in a manner that facilitates easy calculation.

Data availability is probably the most significant obstacle to calculating the effective tax rates of small businesses. Most tax rate studies rely on micro-level (firm level) data to do firm-by-firm comparisons. For corporations, detailed, company-level data on federal income taxes paid is only available on required filings with government regulatory agencies or annual statements provided by the companies. (The IRS does not release company-level federal income tax data to the public.)

Several issues arise when relying on mandatory, corporate filings, such as Form 10-Ks, that are submitted to the Securities and Exchange Commission (SEC). First, only publicly traded corporations are required to file Form 10-K. Second, the population of corporations required to file consists predominantly of large companies. Third, the federal income tax data reported in the 10-Ks may differ in important ways from the taxes actually paid to the Treasury because of differences in financial and tax accounting methods. Fourth, income earned by businesses organized as C corporations is taxed twice, once at the company level and a second time as income is passed along to shareholders in the form of dividend payments or when corporate shares are sold and capital gains are realized. Finally, because corporations represent only a small fraction of total businesses, studies that rely on annual reports and regulatory filings give an incomplete picture of the tax burdens faced by small businesses.

Measuring the tax payments of pass-through entities such as S corporations and partnerships is also a difficult task. Because these business entities don't pay taxes directly – their income and deductions are passed along to their owners and taxed at their owners' rate – published information on the operations of these entities provides little information about the actual taxes these entities incur. Similarly, for the largest group of small businesses in the United States, nonfarm sole proprietorships, accurate and reliable micro-level, federal income tax data do exist, but separating out the actual tax payments accruing to the business from other, non-business related income is challenging.

Nevertheless, a number of studies of effective tax rates can be used as a starting point for examining the issues that face small businesses. Each study has its own strengths and weaknesses, and the studies differ according to entities covered, the calculation of income and taxes, the extent to which small businesses are represented, the data used in the study, and the methodology employed.

A recent study by the Government Accountability Office is representative of the predominant methodology employed in examining the effective tax rates faced by U.S. businesses.[15] The study relied on recently available data collected by the IRS on the domestic and foreign operations of U.S. corporations.[16] The effective tax rate was calculated as the income taxes actually paid by a corporation divided by the corporation's pre-tax, net income. No tax rates were calculated for companies that reported net losses. The study found that the average effective tax rate on domestic income was 25.2 percent. Much lower effective tax rates were found on the foreign-sourced income of U.S. corporations, suggesting that larger multinational firms may have an important advantage over smaller, U.S.-based firms in lowering their effective tax rates. However, there was considerable variation around this average and the results are dominated by large, international corporations. The measure of net income used was income reported for financial purposes (i.e., "book" income) which could differ significantly from a company's taxable income. Parenthetically, the report mentions that effective tax rates can be calculated in different ways that can be used to address different questions. Also, the decision on which measure to use will often depend on conceptual considerations and data availability. A similar version of this methodology was released in 1992 and looked at how corporate income tax rates were affected by the Tax Reform Act of 1986. This study (and a 1990 version of the same study) found that the average effective corporate income tax rate was about 28 percent in 1987, 31.3 percent in 1988, and 37.1 percent in 1989.[17]

Perhaps the study most closely aligned with the current report is a recent examination of how federal tax expenditures affect small businesses.[18] The study did not examine effective tax rates, per se, but looked at how certain tax provisions in the law helped small companies lower their tax bill. This study is important in several respects. It is the first comprehensive examination of how federal tax expenditures affect large and small businesses. The study constructs a proxy measure of a marginal effective income tax rate for these firms. While marginal tax rates can be quite different from effective rates, they are (usually) highly correlated. The study computed estimates of effective tax rates compiled from aggregate data collected by the IRS and supplemented these with case studies that relied on publicly available, company-level data (e.g., 10-K). Because of data availability, the study was limited to C corporations only and, as such, not much can be inferred about the majority of small businesses in the United States. Three business size categories were examined, based on the size of business receipts. The size categories conformed to publicly available data compiled by the IRS: small corporations (less than $5 million), medium-sized corporations ($5 million to $10 million), and large corporations (more than $10 million). Effective tax rates were calculated as the actual income taxes paid divided by taxable income. As such, the income measure in the calculation represents a tax accounting concept and results may differ from those in other studies where financial accounting concepts are used. The methodology used in the study is innovative and demonstrates one important feature of calculating effective tax rates. Each tax expenditure program analyzed was examined separately and in isolation from other tax expenditure programs. As a consequence, there is no interaction assumed among the provisions or on their effect on overall effective tax rates.

Company-specific studies of effective tax rates must rely on publicly available information, and these studies almost always focus on large, publicly traded corporations. Two studies that are representative of this genre are

McIntyre and Nguyen (2000, 2004).[19] Both studies rely on the annual reports and 10-Ks filed with the SEC to develop firm-by-firm estimates of effective tax rates. An effective tax rate for each firm in the study is calculated as current taxes paid divided by net income (i.e., profits) before taxes. Current taxes (a book concept) are calculated by eliminating deferred taxes from the company's reported total tax liability. This measure of current taxes is also reduced by certain tax credits ascertained to have been used from examining each company's tax footnotes that are contained in the annual report to shareholders. In addition, certain types of income that are not included in a company's financial reports (mostly income from employee and executive stock options) are added back in to develop a more comprehensive measure of net income before federal income taxes.[20] Because the focus of these studies is on publicly traded, U.S. corporations, not much can be said about the effective tax rates of small businesses, but the authors suggest that large firms pay effective tax rates that are 6 to 8 percentage points below small firms.

A quite different tack in measuring effective tax rates on businesses is taken in a series of annual studies undertaken by the Congressional Budget Office (CBO, 2007, is representative).[21] Here, the view is that "businesses don't pay taxes, people do," and the studies perform analysis of the incidence of the corporate income tax. In the CBO methodology, U.S. corporate income taxes are allocated to U.S. households based on their holdings of capital assets. The effective tax rate is calculated as corporate income taxes paid (as allocated to U.S. households) divided by total household income. The most recent study finds, using this methodology, that the average effective tax rate for corporations is 2.6 percent. Because the denominator in this study is conceptually different from most other studies of business taxes, the results are not directly comparable, but show how different measures of effective tax rates can be used to answer different questions.

A different measure of an effective tax rate, referred to as the effective marginal tax rate, is useful when looking at the effect of federal income taxes on the decision to invest in new plant and equipment. This measure may be the most relevant, for example, to evaluate how changes in the tax law might affect future economic growth. It is calculated as the single tax rate that would apply to the income stream derived over the life of an asset. As such, the rate is not specific to a particular company, but to a specific tax system (or to the specific tax situation of a representative company). Because the federal income system does not, in general, discriminate between large and small businesses, measures of effective marginal tax rates will, in general, be similar for both groups except to the extent that one group may be able to utilize certain provisions in the tax law not available to the other. For example, the provision that permits expensing of certain business equipment (i.e., Section 179) is phased out when total investment exceeds certain thresholds and, thus, this benefit is generally not utilized by large corporations. Two studies that explore marginal effective tax rates are Gravelle (2003) and CBO (2005).[22] Effective marginal tax rates are similar, conceptually, to estimates of the user cost of capital in that statutory tax rates are adjusted to reflect the timing of certain deductions (e.g., depreciation).

To date, no study has examined the overall federal income tax burden or average effective tax rates faced by small businesses in the United States. This is mostly because the data necessary to support such a study is collected and reported in ways that make it difficult to identify the true tax liabilities of these companies. As a first step to answering this question, this study relies on a methodological approach that combines the conceptual thrust of prior studies – measuring effective tax rates – with powerful simulation tools that help link businesses to owners. This is the first empirical study of its kind.

## V. Description of Federal Income Tax Laws Affecting Small Businesses

### General

Taxes play a critical role in many fundamental economic decisions facing small businesses, including such disparate issues as choice of business form, whether to purchase new equipment, hiring employees, and choice of business location. How a company makes these decisions influences the ultimate rate of federal income tax the business pays.

Small businesses pay a variety of federal taxes, including the following:

1. Income tax, either corporate or individual;
2. Self-employment tax, which is the social security and Medicare tax for individuals who work for themselves;
3. Employment taxes, which are the social security and Medicare taxes for the employees of the business; and
4. Excise taxes, which apply to the manufacture or sale of certain items, the operation of certain kinds of business, the use of certain kinds of

equipment, facilities, or products, and the receipt of payment for certain services.

In addition, federal estate taxes can have the effect of taxing unrealized gains from a business when the business owner dies.

Federal income taxes are imposed on an individual's or a corporation's taxable income. The basic calculation for individuals to compute federal income tax is as follows:

1. Gross income minus deductions from gross income equals adjusted gross income;
2. Adjusted gross income minus itemized deductions or the standard deduction and minus exemptions equals taxable income; and
3. Federal income tax rates applied to taxable income minus credits plus AMT equals net federal income tax due.

The basic calculation for corporations to compute federal income tax is as follows:

1. Gross income minus deductions from gross income and minus special deductions equals taxable income;
2. Federal income tax rates applied to taxable income minus credits (foreign tax credit, credit for federal excise tax on gasoline and special fuels, and combined general business credits); and
3. Net federal income tax is calculated by adding any tax from recomputing prior year's investment credit and any AMT.

By design, a variety of specific federal income tax provisions provide benefits to small businesses generally or to small businesses within specific industries. A listing of these provisions is contained in Appendix B. However, most of the provisions that confer special tax benefits for small businesses apply to a relatively limited class of taxpayers and often are limited to a very narrow industry segment. For example, there is an income tax exemption for very small life insurance companies. While these special provisions may provide significant benefits to the affected businesses, they are unlikely to have a significant effect on overall average effective tax rates for small businesses in general.

This paper examines the burden imposed by federal income taxes on small businesses. The paper does not consider the effects of self-employment taxes, employment taxes, excise taxes, or state and local taxes on small businesses.

Certain provisions of the federal income tax laws are designed to favor small businesses over large businesses. Small businesses are more likely to be structured as flow-through entities, rather than corporations, which results in a single level of federal income tax on business profits. Even if a business is organized as a corporation, the graduated rate structure for corporations provides a benefit to small corporations relative to large corporations. Certain federal tax provisions, such as the provision that allows a specified amount of investment to be expensed rather than depreciated, benefit small businesses relative to large businesses. Finally, there are specific provisions in the federal tax laws that are designed to benefit small businesses in specific industries.[23]

## Business Structure and Federal Income Taxes

How federal income taxes apply to small business income depends upon the business structure selected by the business. Businesses may be operated in a variety of forms and each form may have different federal income tax consequences. There are three primary types of business entities for federal income tax purposes – sole proprietorships, flow-through entities, and corporations. Flow-through entities are not subject to federal income tax, but are instead allowed to "flow" the business profits through to the owners of the business. Corporations, on the other hand, are subject to federal income tax on their income. In addition, the owners of corporations may also be subject to federal income tax on business profits that they receive from the corporation. This is often referred to as the double taxation of corporate profits.

The following summarizes the federal income tax implications of the forms of business commonly utilized by small businesses:

**Sole Proprietorships** – A sole proprietor is an individual who runs an unincorporated business. Sole proprietors are the most familiar and common type of small business in the United States. Sole proprietors report income and deductions on their individual federal income tax returns (Form 1040, Schedule C [Profit or Loss from Business]) or Schedule F [Profit or Loss from Farming]). Sole proprietors can deduct wages and salaries that they pay to their employees, but may not deduct their own salaries or any business income they withdraw from the business.

**Qualified Joint Venture –** An unincorporated business that is owned jointly by a married couple is generally treated as a partnership under the federal tax laws and is required to file a partnership return (see below). Beginning in 2007, however, a married couple could elect to be treated as a "qualified joint venture" and the couple would not have to file as a partnership. The owners of a qualified joint venture report their income and deductions on their individual federal income tax returns (Form 1040, Schedule C [Profit or Loss From Business] or Schedule F [Profit or Loss From Farming]).

**Partnerships –** A partnership is a group of entities (e.g., individuals or businesses) that organize to do business together. Each partner contributes money, property, labor, or skill and shares in the profits of the business. Partnerships are referred to as pass-through entities because the partnership is not separately subject to federal income tax. Instead, income from the partnership is passed-through (allocated) to each partner according to agreed-upon rules and taxed at the partner's tax rate. The partnership files an annual information return (Form 1065) to report the income, deduction, gains, and losses from the business. The individual partners report their partnership income on their individual income tax returns (Form 1040, Schedule E [Supplemental Income and Loss]).

**S Corporations –** S corporations are small business corporations that are afforded the benefits of limited liability (like C corporations – see below) but which can elect to be treated as a pass- through entity for federal income tax purposes. To be eligible for S corporation status, a small business corporation must (1) be a domestic corporation; (2) have no more than 100 shareholders; (3) have shareholders that are only individuals, estates, certain tax-exempt organizations, and certain trusts; (4) have no nonresident alien shareholders; (5) have only one class of stock; (6) not be a bank, insurance company, a possessions corporation, or a domestic international sales corporation; and (7) meet certain other requirements. S corporations must file Form 1120S (U.S. Income Tax Return for an S Corporation), but are exempt from federal income tax other than tax on certain capital gains and passive income.

Individual shareholders of S corporations include their share of the corporation's separately stated items of income, deduction, loss, and credit, and their share of nonseparately stated income or loss on their individual income tax returns (Form 1040, Schedule E [Supplemental Income and Loss]), whether or not the income is distributed to them. Unlike most partnership income, S corporation income is not self-employment income for the S corporation shareholders so the S corporation shareholders are not required to pay self employment taxes with respect to their income. However, distributions and other payments by an S corporation to a corporate officer must be treated as wages to the extent the amounts are reasonable compensation for services rendered for the S corporation.

**Limited Liability Companies (LLC) –** Limited liability companies are relatively new business structures that are authorized under state law. Like owners of a corporation, owners of an LLC have limited personal liability, but other features of an LLC function more like a partnership, such as the flow-through treatment of LLC owner income.

If an LLC has only one owner (referred to as a "member"), the fact that it is an LLC is ignored for federal tax purposes. If the single member is an individual, the LLC income and expenses are reported on Form 1040, Schedule C, E, or F. If the single member is a corporation, the LLC income and expenses are reported on the corporation's return (Form 1120 or Form 1120S). If an LLC has more than one member, most LLC's file a partnership return (Form 1065) and flow through the income and expenses of the LLC to the members. A multiple-member LLC could also elect to be taxed as a corporation.

**C Corporations –** C corporations are formed when prospective shareholders exchange money, property, or both in exchange for capital stock of the C corporation. For federal income tax purposes, a C corporation is a separate taxable entity subject to the corporate income tax. The C corporation is required to file a corporate income tax return (Form 1120 or Form 11 20A) and pay federal corporate income tax on its income. The corporate income is also taxed again to the C corporation shareholders when the income is distributed to them in the form of dividends (reported on Form 1040 and Schedule B) or capital gains (from the sale of their stock or liquidation of the corporation). The C corporation generally is not entitled to deduct the dividends that it distributes to its shareholders.

In some cases, owners of C corporations may receive business profits in the form of compensation for services (wages and salaries). Payments of compensation are generally deductible by the C corporation in computing its federal income tax, but the individual is required to include the income on his or her individual income tax return and the C corporation will be liable for employment taxes with respect to the compensation paid. However, there are rules that prevent a C corporation from paying unreasonable amounts of compensation to its owners. These rules are intended to make sure that the corporate-level tax on business profits is preserved. Thus, a C corporation can only deduct compensation paid to a business owner that is "reasonable."[24]

## Statutory Tax Rates

The U.S. federal income tax system (individual and corporate) uses graduated tax rates that increase as taxable income increases. The 2008 federal individual income tax rates are shown in Tables 18 and 19. These tax rates expire after 2010, when the maximum individual income tax rate will increase to 39.6 percent from the current rate of 35 percent unless the current rate structure is extended.

In addition, a separate temporary rate structure applies to capital gains and dividends, which also expires after 2010. For 2008, the maximum rate of tax on the adjusted net capital gain and certain qualified dividends of an individual is 15 percent (0 percent for individuals whose income would otherwise be taxed at a 10 or 15 percent rate).

Corporations face a maximum income tax rate of 35 percent. Table 20, below, shows the 2008 federal income tax rate schedule for corporations.

**Table 18. 2008 Federal Individual Income Tax Rate Schedule (for Single Individuals)**

| If Taxable Income is Over | But Not Over | The Tax is |
|---|---|---|
| $0 | $8,025 | 10% of the amount over $0 |
| $8,025 | $32,550 | $802.50 plus 15% of the amount over $8,025 |
| $32,550 | $78,850 | $4,481.25 plus 25% of the amount over $32,550 |
| $78,850 | $164,550 | $16,056.25 plus 28% of the amount over $78,850 |
| $164,550 | $357,700 | $40,052.25 plus 33% of the amount over $164,550 |
| $357,700 | no limit | $103,791.75 plus 35% of the amount over $357,700 |

The first two graduated rates described above are phased out for corporations with taxable income between $100,000 and $335,000. As a result, a corporation with taxable income between $335,000 and $10 million effectively is subject to a flat tax rate of 34 percent.

**Table 19. 2008 Federal Individual Income Tax Rate Schedule (for Married Couples Filing a Joint Return)**

| If Taxable Income is Over | But Not Over | The Tax is |
|---|---|---|
| $0 | $16,050 | 10% of the amount over $0 |
| $16,050 | $65,100 | $1,605.00 plus 15% of the amount over $16,050 |
| $65,100 | $131,450 | $8,962.50 plus 25% of the amount over $65,100 |
| $131,450 | $200,300 | $25,550.50 plus 28% of the amount over $131,450 |
| $200,300 | $357,700 | $44,828.00 plus 33% of the amount over $200,300 |
| $357,700 | no limit | $96,770.00 plus 35% of the amount over $357,700 |

**Table 20. 2008 Federal Income Tax Rate Structure for Corporations**

| If Taxable Income Is: | Then the Income Tax Rate Is: |
|---|---|
| $0-$50,000 | 15% |
| $50,001-$75,000 | 25% |
| $75,001-$10 million | 34% |
| Over $10 million | 35% |

Also, the application of the 34 percent rate is phased out for corporations with taxable income between $15 million and $18.3 million, so a corporation with taxable income of $18.3 million or more effectively is subject to a flat rate of 35 percent.

In contrast to the treatment of capital gains in the individual income tax rate structure, no separate rate structure exists for corporate capital gains. Thus, the rate of tax applied to the net capital gains of a corporation is 35 percent.

## Alternative Minimum Tax

In addition to the regular income tax rates, small businesses are also affected by the alternative minimum tax (AMT) on individuals and corporations. The tax laws give preferential treatment to certain kinds of income and allow special deductions and credits for certain kinds of expenses. The alternative minimum tax (AMT) attempts to ensure that anyone who benefits from these tax advantages pays at least a minimum amount of tax.

Thus, the AMT is designed to provide a backstop to the regular income tax so that deductions and credits cannot reduce the amount of federal income tax paid below a minimum level.

The AMT is a separately figured tax that eliminates many deductions and credits, thus increasing tax liability for an individual who would otherwise pay less tax. The tentative minimum tax rates on ordinary income are percentages set by law. For individuals, the AMT tax rate is either 26 percent or 28 percent and applies in addition to the regular income tax. For capital gains and certain dividends, the rates in effect for the regular tax (0 percent and 15 percent) are used. There is an exemption amount that is designed to make sure that lower income taxpayers are not subject to the AMT. While the individual AMT was originally intended to apply primarily to high-income individuals, it increasingly is affecting middle-income individuals as well.[25]

Corporations are also subject to an AMT. The AMT rate for corporations is 20 percent. Small corporations with average gross receipts of less than $7.5 million for all three-year tax periods prior to the current year are exempt from the corporate AMT. In addition, new corporations are not subject to the AMT for their first year of existence, regardless of their receipts.

## Deductions

Individuals and corporations reduce their federal income tax liability through the use of deductions and credits. The use of these deductions and credits can have a big effect on a small business's effective federal income tax rate.

All taxpayers (corporate and individual) are entitled to deduct from gross income the ordinary and necessary expenses of carrying on a trade or business. Among these ordinary and necessary business expenses are such items as salaries and wages, utilities, rent, advertising, legal and accounting expenses, and car and truck expenses.

An expense that adds to the value or useful life of property is considered a capital expense and is not deductible as an ordinary and necessary business expense. Instead, the general rule is that a capital expense must be deducted through depreciation, amortization, or depletion. Deductions for depreciable assets occur over the life of the asset under special rules.

However, a business that has limited investments in certain depreciable business assets may elect to expense the assets (i.e., deduct currently) rather than claiming depreciation deductions over the life of the asset. This expensing provision, referred to as Section 179 expensing, benefits primarily small businesses. For 2008, the maximum amount that can be expensed is $250,000. After 2010, the maximum dollar amount of the expensing deduction reverts to $25,000 per year unless the treatment under current law is extended. If a business purchases more than $800,000 (for 2008) of qualified property, the special expensing deduction is reduced dollar for dollar by the businesses investment in excess of $800,000.

Section 179 expensing reduces the cost of capital for small businesses and reduces tax compliance costs by eliminating the need for these businesses to calculate depreciation deductions and keep track of the cost basis of their assets.

In some cases, limitations on deductions may adversely affect small businesses. For example, the deduction for business-related meals and entertainment expenses is limited to 50 percent of the expense. Meals and entertainment can represent a disproportionately larger share of a small business's expenses relative to larger businesses and the limitation on the deduction limits the ability of a small business to offset federal tax liability by the amount of these expenses.

## Health Insurance, Retirement Plans, and Other Employee Benefits

The federal tax system generally treats compensation provided in the form of certain employee benefits as either nontaxable (i.e., excluded from gross income) or tax deferred. Employer- provided health insurance is generally not taxed as compensation to employees. Employer- provided retirement savings is generally tax deferred; employees can defer the tax on their qualified retirement savings until they retire.

It is important to remember that these tax incentives apply to employees, rather than employers. The costs of employee benefits are generally the same as compensation costs and are deductible to the employer as ordinary and necessary business expenses. As a result, employers should generally be indifferent from a federal tax perspective as to whether to pay employees in current compensation or to provide them with health, retirement, or other employee benefits.

However, employers often prefer to provide employee benefits in lieu of compensation for a variety of reasons. Employees often prefer to receive compensation in a nontaxable or tax deferred form and providing these benefits may help employers attract and retain their workforce. The federal tax system provides the strongest incentive for retirement saving to occur through an employer-sponsored qualified retirement plan system. There is a substantially higher limit on the amount of permissible tax-qualified retirement savings if the savings occurs through an employer-sponsored plan.

Despite these incentives, small businesses are much less likely to provide health insurance and qualified retirement plans to their employees. In the case of health insurance, the costs of providing coverage for a small business may be prohibitive because small employers cannot qualify for the economies of scale and risk pooling that occur with large employers.[26]

Self-employed individuals are entitled to deduct 100 percent of their health insurance expenses during a year for income tax purposes, but not for social security and Medicare tax purposes. This has the effect, for federal income tax purposes, of treating self-employed individuals the same as employees who work for an employer that provides health insurance benefits.

In the case of qualified retirement plans, the costs of establishing and maintaining a plan can create a significant deterrent to small and mid-sized employers. Once established, the plan must meet standards for participation and nondiscrimination so that the benefits are generally available to all eligible employees, regardless of income or ability to save. In the case of defined benefit pension plans, the plan also must satisfy annual minimum funding requirements. The costs of complying with these minimum funding requirements are significant. Changes to the rules for qualified retirement plans occur with alarming frequency. Thus, employers are constantly facing the costs of amending their plans to comply with new laws and regulations.

In recent years, Congress has recognized that the incentives of current law may not be sufficient to induce small businesses to establish and continue qualified retirement plans. Thus, Congress has passed additional laws to assist smaller employers, offered alternatives to defined benefit plans, and expanded existing retirement savings options. The available plans from which employers may choose each have detailed rules on participation and contributions, creating a very complex system.[27]

## Summary of Federal Income Taxes That Apply to Small Business Owners

Table 21, below, summarizes the application of federal income taxes to small businesses based on the form of the business. Sole proprietorships are the most common form of small business, but represent a relatively small percentage of total business receipts. While the corporate form provides the advantage of limited personal liability, small businesses often avoid the corporate form of business because of the double taxation of business profits. The rise of limited liability companies provides small businesses with the best of both worlds by providing limited personal liability and flow-through tax treatment so that only one level of tax is applied to business profits.

# VI. METHODOLOGY FOR MEASURING EFFECTIVE TAX RATES

## Importance of Effective Tax Rates

Under the federal income tax system, a progressive statutory rate structure applies to income of businesses and individuals. The income of C corporations is taxed twice, once at the corporate level through the payment of the corporate income tax and again to the individual owner of a corporation when corporate profits are distributed in the form of dividends or capital gains. Other forms of business, such as sole proprietorships, partnerships, and S corporations, are not subject to an entity level tax and business profits are taxed only to the individual owners of the business.

As a result, figuring out the overall costs of federal income taxes to small business owners requires an examination of both corporate and individual income taxes to explore who bears the burden of the taxes on business income. In addition, exceptions to the normal tax rules (e.g., deductions, exclusions, and credits) can have the effect of lowering the overall rate of tax imposed. On the other hand, the alternative minimum tax (AMT) can have the effect of increasing the overall rate of tax paid. Thus, there is a difference between the statutory rate of tax and the effective tax rates that small businesses (and small business owners) face. Effective tax rates provide a more accurate picture of how taxes are imposed on small businesses.

Most of the research done to date examines the effect of federal taxes imposed directly by the corporate income tax. Because most small businesses do not pay federal income taxes directly – their income, losses and deductions are passed through to their owners – federal income tax liabilities cannot be directly ascertained for these business types. As such, the existing research that examines the tax burden of small businesses is necessarily incomplete.

**Table 21. Summary of Application of Federal Income Taxes to Small Businesses**

| Form of Business | Individual Income Tax | Corporate Income Tax |
|---|---|---|
| Sole Proprietorship | Applies | Does not apply |
| Qualified Joint Venture (married couple) | Applies to each spouse's share of income | Does not apply |
| Partnership | Applies to each partner's share of partnership income | Does not apply |
| S Corporation | Applies to shareholder's share of S corporation income | Does not apply unless S corporation elects to be taxed as a corporation |
| Limited Liability Company (LLC) | Applies to member's share of LLC income | Does not apply unless LLC elects to be taxed as a corporation |
| C corporation | Applies to dividends paid to shareholders | Applies |

## Microsimulation

This study relies on microsimulation to calculate the effective tax rates of small businesses in the U.S. For more than thirty years, microsimulation has been a workhorse of tax policy analysis. In this modeling approach, aggregate outcomes are simulated from the "bottom-up," by focusing on the micro-level components of the tax system (e.g., individuals or businesses).

In microsimulation, federal income taxes are simulated for each taxpayer by means of a very detailed tax calculator that incorporates the parameters and features of the current tax law. Quite often, the analyst is also interested in how a change in one or more aspects of existing tax law may affect revenues or the distribution of income taxes. This counterfactual simulation is then compared with estimates of tax liabilities under the original, or baseline simulation.

## Data Sources

In order to examine the effect of federal income taxes on small business owners more accurately, this paper explores corporations, pass-through entities like partnerships and S corporations, and sole proprietorships. The challenge is tracing business income in a way that accurately captures the full effect of the federal income tax system for each type of small business entity.

The principal data source is a sample of individual federal income tax returns representative of all individual returns filed in 2004, the most recent year for which firm-level data are available. The IRS Individual Statistics of Income Public Use File (PUF) is an annual, micro-level data file constructed from a stratified, random sample of approximately150,000 U.S. taxpayers. Stratification is done with respect to income and income sources; wealthy, high-income individuals are over-sampled. The PUF contains detailed information on the income, deductions, tax credits and tax liabilities of all individual tax filers in the United States. The incomes reported include income from sole proprietorships as well as income from partnerships (including LLCs) and S Corporations.

Small businesses interact with the federal income tax system in different ways. For the most common type of small business in the United States, nonfarm sole proprietorships, business income and deductions are reported along with other types of income on the individual income tax return (i.e., Form 1040) on Schedule C relating to business income or loss. This income is combined with other types of income that the business owner might have received (e.g., interest and dividend income) that may or may not be directly related to the business operations. The total income received by the taxpayer, after appropriate adjustments, is then taxed according to the tax laws in place for each tax year. While accurate, aggregate estimates of the amount of sole proprietor income received by individual business owners can be ascertained from published IRS sources, no estimate of the actual tax liabilities incurred by the businesses can be calculated without additional information on the taxpayers and their sources of income. Microsimulation permits the isolation of the amount of federal income tax that is attributable to the business.

For small businesses organized as partnerships or S corporations, the situation is more complicated. These businesses are required to file federal income tax returns that state the nature of the business, the income and deductions claimed, and the amount of net income that is passed along to the business owners according to their ownership stakes on Form 1065 (partnerships) or Form 1120-S (S corporations). No federal income tax liability is assessed on these tax returns.[28] However, the net income is reported on the income tax returns of the owners on Schedule E (Supplemental Income), relating to income from rental property, royalties, S corporations, partnerships and trusts. By identifying the income from these business sources, the federal income taxes incurred by the business can be estimated using a microsimulation model.

C corporations pay federal income taxes directly and small businesses that are organized this way report their tax liability separately on Form 1120, the primary tax form for U.S. corporations. While no publicly available, micro-level, federal income tax data exist for corporations, the IRS annually compiles detailed tabulations of corporation information in the Corporate Source Book , an annual summary of the income, deductions, credits, taxes and financial data (i.e., asset size). These tabulations can be used to estimate the federal income tax liability and effective tax rate of these entities.

## Summary of Methodology Employed to Measure Effective Tax Rates

Quantria Strategies' proprietary individual income tax microsimulation model is the primary tool used to calculate effective tax rates. The model uses the 2004 PUF as its principal data source with supplemental data provided by the 2004 Corporate Source Book (CSB). For non-corporate businesses and S corporations, total federal income tax liability is calculated for each tax return in the PUF sample based on a detailed specification of the tax law in place for 2004. In the microsimulation model, results for each individual tax record are then aggregated to arrive at national totals.[29] This specification of the tax law includes all the adjustments, exemptions, exclusions, tax credits and income phase-outs that are part of calculating total federal income tax liability. The tax calculations in the model have been tested extensively and validated; they reproduce actual tax liabilities reported by U.S. taxpayers for tax year 2004 to within approximately 1 percent.

Small businesses are identified in the model based upon whether or not they report income (or losses) from sole proprietorships (Schedule C, Profit or Loss from Business), partnerships (Schedule E, Supplemental Income or Loss, Part II) or S corporations (Schedule E, Supplemental Income or Loss, Part II).[30] Taxpayers who operate more than one business of a single entity type have their income aggregated over all businesses in the PUF sample. For taxpayers who report income from more than one business entity type, each source of income is treated as a unique business and separate calculations are performed in the simulations. Businesses without net income are ignored to avoid distorting the calculations.

Operationally, the effective tax rate of each small business in the sample is calculated by performing two simulations. In the first simulation (the "baseline"), the total tax liability of each small business taxpayer is calculated under the tax laws and rules in place for 2004. It is important to note that this tax liability will usually include taxes paid on other, non-business sources of income such as interest income. In the second simulation (the "alternative policy"), net income accruing to the business is isolated for each business entity type and the federal income tax liability is recalculated after subtracting this income from the taxpayer's total income. The resulting change in tax liability (which in this case will be negative, reflecting the fact that income has been reduced) is an estimate of the taxes attributable to the small business.[31] For taxpayers whose only source of income is small business income, this calculation gives the correct result: all federal income tax liability is assigned to the business since no federal income taxes will be due on zero net income. The estimate of the effective tax rate faced by the business is then calculated as the change in tax liability[32] divided by the net income (before taxes) of the business. The estimates of effective tax rates reported here are aggregate estimates, averaged across all small businesses in the reporting group. For example, when reporting an effective tax rate for a particular business entity type, the numerator is the (weighted) sum of the calculated tax changes attributable to the businesses while the denominator is the (weighted) sum of the net incomes of the businesses.

For nonfarm sole proprietorships, representing over 70 percent of small businesses in the United States, the information contained on Schedule C in the PUF is very detailed and includes:

Net receipts
Cost of goods sold
Other income
Depreciation
Insurance
Mortgage interest
Other interest expense
Office expenses
Net wages
Total deductions

For S corporation and partnerships, the information is somewhat more general but includes both active and passive income and loss amounts, as well as the Section 179 expense deduction. To calculate the effective tax rates of C corporations, tabular, or cell-based data contained in the 2004 Corporate Source Book is utilized. A more detailed description of the methodology is contained in Appendix A.

## Limitations on Data and Methodology

While microsimulation is the only method available that can provide an accurate picture of the tax burden facing all small businesses in the United States, there are some important qualifications to this analysis.

First, the methodology imposes an implied "stacking order" in the calculation of small business tax liability by assuming that small business income is taxed last. Because the federal income tax rate structure is progressive, stacking business income last will reflect a higher marginal tax rate than if the business income was stacked first. Thus, this stacking will tend to slightly overestimate the tax liability of those business owners who receive large amounts of other, non- business income.

Second and closely related to the first, is that this methodology treats as separate entities multiple businesses owned by the same taxpayer.[33] This approach identifies the effective tax rate associated with each business, but not necessarily the overall effective tax rate faced by the owner of the business.

Third, the effective tax rates are calculated only for U.S. business owners that are taxed as individuals. To the extent some business owners (e.g., partners or S corporation shareholders) are non-U.S. citizens or other entity types, then the income accruing to these entities is not counted.[34]

Fourth, the income of C corporations is taxed twice, once at the business level and once again when income is passed along to owners and investors, either as dividend payments or capital gain realizations. While the individual income tax data does contain information on the dividends and capital gains of taxpayers, there is no reliable method to allocate these amounts to small businesses. Thus, the effective tax rate analysis does not capture the taxes paid by C corporation owners on dividends and capital gains. This will tend to understate somewhat the total effective tax rate of small businesses organized as C corporations, but this bias will tend to be small, particularly because of the fairly low rates of tax currently applicable to individual dividends and capital gains.

Fifth, to the extent small business owners receive a salary from the business – which may be the case for C corporations – then there is no reliable way to identify those payments and calculate the income taxes paid on them from existing data. Conceptually, it makes sense to ignore these payments because they are, in theory, equivalent to what the individual business owner would receive if he or she were an employee of another business. However, because salary and wage payments are deductible to C corporations, a C corporation owner may attempt to withdraw business profits in the form of a salary to avoid the corporate-level income tax. There are existing rules to prevent this by denying deductions for unreasonable compensation.

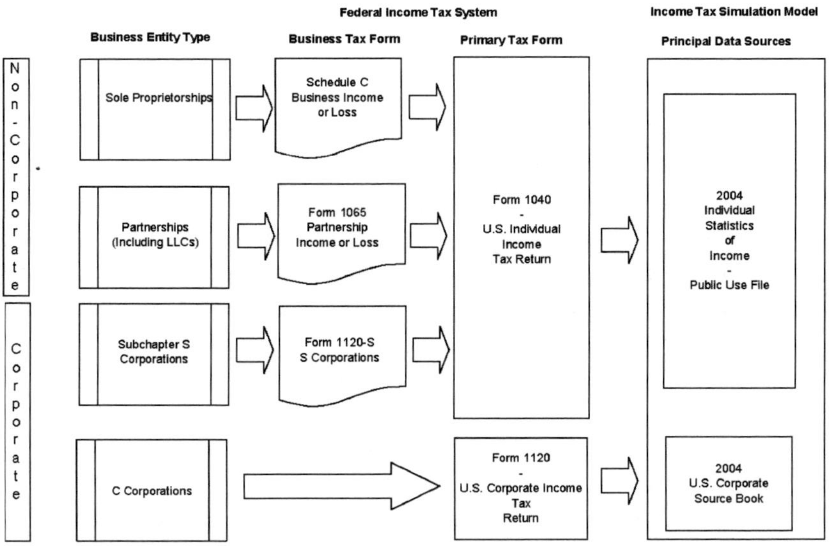


Figure 1. Schematic of Federal Income Tax Flows and Calculation of Effective Tax Rates

Finally, it is important to remember that there are a variety of special tax provisions applicable to small businesses for federal income tax purposes.[35] These provisions often provide a special tax benefit for small businesses in a specific industry. For the affected taxpayers, these provisions can have a significant effect on effective tax rates. However, because the scope of these provisions is often quite narrow, their overall impact on the average effective tax rates of small businesses will likely be quite small.

Figure 1 summarizes how small businesses interact with the federal income tax system, the forms and schedules that are filed, how the data are collected and how these data are used to calculate effective tax rates in the simulation model.

# VII. Results: Effective Tax Rates Faced by Small Businesses

Small businesses in the United States pay an estimated average effective tax rate of approximately 19.8 percent. This figure is derived from the Quantria Strategies, LLC individual income tax microsimulation model of individual taxpayers, supplemented with selected tabular, cell-based data on the net income and taxes of C corporations. The use of microsimulation permits the accurate measurement of the tax liabilities reported on individual income tax returns by sole proprietors, partners of partnerships, and shareholders of S corporations.

A great deal of variation in effective tax rates exists across business entity types. S corporations pay the highest effective tax rate. As discussed below, the effective tax rate for C corporations is not directly comparable to the effective tax rates of other entities for a variety of reasons. Table 22 summarizes the effective tax rate calculations for small businesses by entity type.

As explained in the previous section, these calculations are performed only for small businesses with positive net income.[36]

It is useful to examine how the overall effective tax rate varies by size of net income. This measure will indicate the relative progressivity of the tax system and give a better feel for the magnitude of the federal income tax burden by the size of the business. Table 23 breaks down the taxes paid by nonfarm sole proprietorships. It shows that, for 2004, most small businesses earned less than $10,000 in net income and paid roughly 8.1 percent of this in income taxes. Tax burdens, generally, rise slightly with net income and the largest sole proprietors, with net income above $200,000, pay the highest average effective rate of tax, almost 24 percent. This figure is close to what some studies estimate to be the average effective tax rate of a large U.S. corporation.

**Table 22. Effective Tax Rate Summary, by Entity Type, 2004**

| Entity Type | Number of Taxpayers* | Net Income ($million) | Change in Taxes ($million) | Effective Tax Rate |
|---|---|---|---|---|
| Non Farm Sole Proprietorships | 14,910,181 | $283,307.8 | $37,737.9 | 13.3% |
| Partnerships | 1,445,452 | 127,163.3 | 29,958.8 | 23.6% |
| S Corporations | 2,328,104 | 209,183.2 | 56,252.9 | 26.9% |
| C Corporations | 899,508 | 49,534.0 | 8,693.0 | 17.5% |
| **All Small Businesses** | **19,583,245** | **$699,188.4** | **$132,642.6** | **19.8%** |

* Businesses with net income

Source: Quantria Strategies, LLC Individual Income Tax Simulation Model, IRS Individual Income Tax Public Use File, 2004, and IRS Corporate Source Book, 2004.

**Table 23. Estimated Effective Tax Rates for Nonfarm Sole Proprietorships, by Size of Net Income, 2004**

| Size of Net Income | Number of Taxpayers with a Change in Federal Income Tax Liability | Net Income ($million) | Change in Taxes ($million) | Effective Tax Rate |
|---|---|---|---|---|
| Less than $10,000 | 8,923,483 | $31,735.2 | $2,584.6 | 8.1% |
| $10,001 to $20,000 | 2,647,899 | 37,467.0 | 2,555.6 | 6.8% |
| $20,001 to $30,000 | 1,166,843 | 28,587.7 | 2,318.2 | 8.1% |
| $30,001 to $40,000 | 607,497 | 20,956.3 | 1,983.8 | 9.5% |
| $40,001 to $50,000 | 396,378 | 17,656.3 | 1,815.6 | 10.3% |
| $50,001 to $75,000 | 451,207 | 27,407.6 | 3,372.0 | 12.3% |
| $75,001 to $100,000 | 253,250 | 21,752.2 | 3,025.7 | 13.9% |
| $100,001 to $200,000 | 318,918 | 44,410.7 | 7,348.6 | 16.5% |
| $200,000 or more | 144,706 | 53,334.8 | 12,733.8 | 23.9% |
| **Total All Returns** | **14,910,181** | **$283,307.8** | **$37,737.9** | **13.3%** |

Source: Quantria Strategies, LLC Individual Income Tax Simulation Model and IRS Individual Income Tax Public Use File, 2004.

Table 24 shows the same breakdown of federal income taxes for businesses that are formed as partnerships. While the tax structure is generally progressive for partnerships, there are some noticeable gaps. The lowest income group pays a tax rate that is higher than all but the two highest groups. This could be the case, for example, if partnership income were a small fraction of a taxpayer's total income. Because the microsimulation model assumes that business income is effectively taxed last, this may overstate the effective tax rate for these taxpayer groups.

**Table 24. Estimated Effective Tax Rates for Partnerships, by Size of Net Income, 2004**

| Size of Net Income | Number of Taxpayers with a Change in Federal Income Tax Liability | Net Income ($million) | Change in Taxes ($million) | Effective Tax Rate |
|---|---|---|---|---|
| Less than $10,000 | 610,432 | $1,688.4 | $281.4 | 16.7% |
| $10,001 to $20,000 | 161,513 | 2,351.0 | 325.2 | 13.8% |
| $20,001 to $30,000 | 116,691 | 2,920.7 | 383.7 | 13.1% |
| $30,001 to $40,000 | 82,761 | 2,849.2 | 412.8 | 14.5% |
| $40,001 to $50,000 | 52,539 | 2,328.0 | 371.3 | 16.0% |
| $50,001 to $75,000 | 92,119 | 5,682.2 | 807.6 | 14.2% |
| $75,001 to $100,000 | 56,118 | 4,859.0 | 746.1 | 15.4% |
| $100,001 to $200,000 | 113,824 | 15,859.5 | 3,061.0 | 19.3% |
| $200,000 or more | 159,456 | 88,625.2 | 23,569.6 | 26.6% |
| **Total All Returns** | **1,445,453** | **$127,163.2** | **$29,958.7** | **23.6%** |

Source: Quantria Strategies, LLC Individual Income Tax Simulation Model and IRS Individual Income Tax Public Use File, 2004.

Table 25 examines S corporations, the entity type that is estimated to pay the highest average effective tax rate among small businesses. A close examination of the table suggests that this may have more to do with the distribution of net income of S corporation owners, with much of the income accruing to the largest firms.

Contrast the somewhat high effective tax rates incurred by S corporations with the lower effective tax rates estimated for businesses organized as C corporations. There may be several reasons for this. First, it is common for the owners of small C corporations to receive a salary from the business. This salary would be deductible to the C corporation (and reduce C corporation federal income tax liability) unless the payment constituted unreasonable compensation. The salary would be subject to tax on the C corporation owner's individual income tax return and these federal income tax payments theoretically should be attributable to the business. However, existing data do not allow these payments to be traced to the owners of C corporations, so the tax on salary payments is not captured in this analysis.

Second, corporate income is also taxed when it is distributed to shareholders in the form of dividends or capital gains. Again, the existing data do not permit the tracing of C corporation owners in order to capture these federal income tax effects.

**Table 25. Estimated Effective Tax Rates for S Corporations, by Size of Net Income, 2004**

| Size of Net Income | Number of Taxpayers with a Change in Federal Income Tax Liability | Net Income ($million) | Change in Taxes ($million) | Effective Tax Rate |
|---|---|---|---|---|
| Less than $10,000 | 707,805 | $2,702.7 | $419.3 | 15.5% |
| $10,001 to $20,000 | 324,019 | 4,716.3 | 745.7 | 15.8% |
| $20,001 to $30,000 | 214,044 | 5,269.0 | 849.9 | 16.1% |
| $30,001 to $40,000 | 175,084 | 6,038.2 | 984.5 | 16.3% |
| $40,001 to $50,000 | 157,186 | 6,945.0 | 1,043.9 | 15.0% |
| $50,001 to $75,000 | 203,374 | 12,444.5 | 2,220.9 | 17.8% |
| $75,001 to $100,000 | 121,004 | 10,547.0 | 2,187.3 | 20.7% |
| $100,001 to $200,000 | 215,951 | 30,217.6 | 7,061.1 | 23.4% |
| $200,000 or more | 209,636 | 130,303.0 | 40,740.4 | 3 1.3% |
| **Total All Returns** | **2,328,103** | **$209,183.3** | **$56,252.9** | **26.9%** |

Source: Quantria Strategies, LLC Individual Income Tax Simulation Model, IRS Individual Income Tax Public Use File, 2004, and IRS Corporate Source Book, 2004.

**Table 26. Estimated Effective Tax Rates for C Corporations, by Size of Assets, 2004**

| Size of Assets | Number of Taxpayers with a Change in Federal Income Tax Liability | Net Income ($million) | Change in Taxes ($million) | Effective Tax Rate |
|---|---|---|---|---|
| Less than $500,000 | 669,313 | $15,118.7 | $1,603.7 | 10.6% |
| $500,001 to $1 million | 100,336 | 6,453.6 | 976.7 | 15.1% |
| $1,000,001 to $5 million | 112,076 | 18,260.9 | 3,613.0 | 19.8% |
| $5,000,001 to $10 million | 17,783 | 9,700.8 | 2,499.6 | 25.8% |
| **Total All Returns** | **899,508** | **$49,534.0** | **$8,693.0** | **17.5%** |

Source: Quantria Strategies, LLC Individual Income Tax Simulation Model and IRS Corporate Source Book, 2004.

Table 26 summarizes the results for C corporations. The figures in Table 26 are not directly comparable to those presented for other tax entity types because no micro-level data on the incomes and taxes of corporations are available. As such, published data from the 2004 Corporation Source Book is used to perform the calculations. One difference in the figures concerns the size category used to classify taxpayers. Aggregate federal income tax data for C corporations is generally only available by asset size.[37]

**Table 27. Estimated Effective Tax Rates for Nonfarm Sole Proprietorships by Industry, 2004**

| Industry Sector | Number of Taxpayers with a Change in Federal Income Tax Liability | Net Income ($million) | Change in Taxes ($million) | Effective Tax Rate |
|---|---|---|---|---|
| Agriculture | 180,961 | $2,363.8 | $262.3 | 11.7% |
| Mining | 103,680 | 1,858.4 | 236.0 | 12.7% |
| Utilities | 7,362 | 95.8 | 3.9 | 4.1% |
| Construction | 1,865,705 | 38,541.1 | 5,047.8 | 13.1% |
| Manufacturing | 219,685 | 3,850.6 | 479.9 | 12.5% |
| Wholesale & Retail Trade | 2,115,767 | 38,922.8 | 5,536.8 | 14.2% |
| Transportation & Warehousing | 740,640 | 17,098.7 | 2,266.0 | 13.3% |
| Information | 173,429 | 3,148.8 | 379.1 | 12.0% |
| Finance, Insurance & Real Estate | 1,393,845 | 34,737.7 | 4,839.9 | 13.9% |
| Professional, Scientific & Technical Services | 2,247,993 | 41,743.2 | 5,387.4 | 12.9% |
| Other Services | 5,861,116 | 100,947.0 | 13,298.7 | 13.2% |
| **Total All Returns** | **14,910,183** | **$283,307.9** | **$37,737.8** | **13.3%** |

Source: Quantria Strategies, LLC Individual Income Tax Simulation Model and IRS Individual Income Tax Public Use File, 2004.

To the extent that different industries can lower their effective tax burden by utilizing special provisions in the tax law or have access to additional tax planning opportunities not available to other companies, then their effective tax rates should be lower. However, as noted earlier in this report, many of the existing special tax provisions for specific industries benefit relatively narrow classes of businesses.

**Table 28. Estimated Effective Tax Rates for Partnerships, by Industry, 2004**

| Industry Sector | Number of Taxpayers with a Change in Federal Income Tax Liability | Net Income ($million) | Change in Taxes ($million) | Effective Tax Rate |
|---|---|---|---|---|
| Agriculture | 79,753 | $4,063.5 | $868.8 | 21.4% |
| Mining | 14,020 | 1,347 | 330.1 | 24.5% |
| Utilities | 1,537 | 108.5 | 23 | 21.2% |
| Construction | 79,789 | 7,545.2 | 1,834.9 | 24.3% |
| Manufacturing | 31,578 | 2,317.5 | 515.9 | 22.3% |
| Wholesale & Retail Trade | 102,413 | 9,197.6 | 2,221.7 | 24.2% |
| Transportation & Warehousing | 14,918 | 1,593.8 | 361.8 | 22.7% |
| Information | 24,828 | 1,735.2 | 430.5 | 24.8% |
| Finance, Insurance & Real Estate | 819,709 | 74,225.4 | 17,448.1 | 23.5% |
| Professional, Scien-tific & Technical Services | 101,932 | 9,334.8 | 2,293.4 | 24.6% |
| Other Services | 174,973 | 15,694.8 | 3,630.5 | 23.1% |
| **Total All Returns** | **1,445,450** | **$127,163.3** | **$29,958.7** | **23.6%** |

Source: Quantria Strategies, LLC Individual Income Tax Simulation Model and IRS Individual Income Tax Public Use File, 2004.

Further, the SOI Public Use File does not contain industry-level micro-data that can be used in the microsimulation model. An attempt is made to overcome this lack of detail by imputing the industry of the taxpayer in order to examine how taxes may be affected. As a consequence, the analysis presented in Tables 27 through 30 is only suggestive of how effective tax rates might vary by industry group and should be used with caution.

For nonfarm sole proprietors, partnerships and S corporations, little variation occurs across industries in estimated effective tax rates. The imputation methodology and lack of sufficient data to impute industries accurately may contribute to this uniformity. On the other hand, a similar effect is observed for C corporations with very little variation in the effective tax rates across industries. Clearly, more detailed micro-level data are needed to ascertain how specific industries may be affected by the federal income tax system.

In summary, small businesses in the United States pay a significant share of federal income taxes. For most companies, those that are organized as sole proprietorships, the effective tax rate is quite low, but this is primarily because most of these businesses earn so little income.

**Table 29. Estimated Effective Tax Rates for S Corporations, by Industry, 2004**

| Industry Sector | Number of Taxpayers with a Change in Federal Income Tax Liability | Net Income ($million) | Change in Taxes ($million) | Effective Tax Rate |
|---|---|---|---|---|
| Agriculture | 79,761 | $4,470.1 | $1,119.7 | 25.0% |
| Mining | 10,376 | 960.4 | 278.1 | 29.0% |
| Utilities | 4,018 | 315.5 | 77.5 | 24.6% |
| Construction | 300,132 | 28,428.1 | 7,759.2 | 27.3% |
| Manufacturing | 82,320 | 8,756.8 | 2,342.2 | 26.7% |
| Wholesale & Retail Trade | 371,564 | 33,203.3 | 8,887.2 | 26.8% |
| Transportation & Wareho-using | 78,801 | 6,509.1 | 1,794.3 | 27.6% |
| Information | 46,546 | 4,048.9 | 1,075.5 | 26.6% |
| Finance, Insur-ance & Real Estate | 371,290 | 33,786.0 | 8,817.3 | 26.1% |
| Professional, Scientific, & Technical Ser-vices | 357,471 | 32,527.2 | 8,855.0 | 27.2% |
| Other Services | 625,824 | 56,178.2 | 15,246.9 | 27.1% |
| **Total All Returns** | **2,328,103** | **$209,183.6** | **$56,252.9** | **26.9%** |

Source: Quantria Strategies, LLC Individual Income Tax Simulation Model, IRS Individual Income Tax Public Use File, 2004, and IRS Corporate Source Book, 2004.

**Table 30. Estimated Effective Tax Rates for C Corporations by Industry, 2004**

| Industry Sector | Number of Taxpayers with a Change in Federal Income Tax Liability | Net Income ($million) | Change in Taxes ($million) | Effective Tax Rate |
|---|---|---|---|---|
| Agriculture | 33,291 | 1,759.5 | $227.7 | 12.9% |
| Mining | 6,316 | 657.4 | 132.9 | 20.2% |
| Utilities | 1,538 | 284.6 | 77.1 | 27.1% |
| Construction | 103,367 | 5,869.1 | 955.0 | 16.3% |
| Manufacturing | 54,706 | 6,268.8 | 1,224.3 | 19.5% |
| Wholesale & Retail Trade | 193,954 | 10,586.9 | 2,100.8 | 19.8% |
| Transportation & Warehousing | 29,258 | 1,671.3 | 276.1 | 16.5% |
| Information | 18,134 | 1,515.8 | 233.4 | 15.4% |
| Finance, Insurance & Real Estate | 137,134 | 8,337.9 | 1,531.6 | 18.4% |
| Professional, Scientific & Technical Services | 108,268 | 5,812.6 | 1,045.2 | 18.0% |
| Other Services | 213,542 | 6,770.3 | 888.7 | 13.1% |
| **Total All Returns** | **899,508** | **$49,534.0** | **$8,693.0** | **17.5%** |

Source: Quantria Strategies, LLC Individual Income Tax Simulation Model and IRS Corporate Source Book, 2004.

Partnerships and S corporations pay the highest rates among small businesses – with S corporations paying the highest. This is quite likely a result of their relatively larger size. C corporations pay the lowest rate of tax according to this analysis. Caution should be used when interpreting this result because the measurement tools are somewhat imprecise when tracing the ultimate taxes paid by C corporations.

# Appendix A. Technical Description of the Study Methodology

This Appendix provides additional, technical details on the methodology used in this study to estimated effective tax rates for small businesses. The Appendix (1) describes Quantria Strategies' proprietary microsimulation model; (2) explains how the model identifies and simulates the federal income tax liability for different business entity types; (3) documents the assumptions used in the effective tax rate calculations; and (4) discusses the limitations that apply to the effective tax rate analysis.

## Individual Income Tax Microsimulation Model

Quantria Strategies, LLC maintains a detailed microsimulation model of the U.S. individual federal income tax system. Microsimulation models have been used in tax policy analysis for more than thirty years and provide policymakers with the necessary tools and information to make informed decisions about the costs and impacts of tax law changes. By focusing on the micro units in the economy, microsimulation calculates aggregate outcomes from the "bottom- up." In this case, the micro units are individual taxpayers and the analysis characterizes changes in their federal income tax liability under alternative policy scenarios.

While microsimulation is the primary tool in examining the effect of alternative tax policy options, it is frequently used in conjunction with other types of economic models such as large, multi-sector models of the macroeconomy and computable general equilibrium (CGE) models. Each modeling approach has its own strengths and weaknesses and the choice of one over another will usually depend on the types of questions one is trying to answer. Microsimulation is usually the preferred analytical method when the tax policy options being investigated exhibit some degree of non-linearity resulting in complex interactions among the provisions, or when distribution analysis – examining which taxpayer groups are affected disproportionately under a proposed tax change – is important.

Central to the microsimulation model is a detailed description of the tax law in place (e.g., the tax calculator). This allows the analyst to vary certain tax law parameters and examine how tax liability varies under the new regime on a taxpayer-by-taxpayer basis. Mechanically, one generally performs two simulations: a calculation of tax liability under present law (the "baseline") and a second simulation for some proposed policy option (the "alternative"). The difference in tax liability represents the effect of the proposal, and this effect, calculated over all taxpayers, represents the aggregate effect of the law change. Because changes in tax liability are calculated at the micro level, the analyst can examine how different taxpayer segments are affected by the change. For example, it is customary to examine changes by income classes, filing types (e.g., single taxpayers versus married couples), and whether the taxpayer itemizes his or her deductions.

## Data Sources

The principal data source in the present version of the Quantria microsimulation model is the 2004 Statistics of Income (SOI) Public Use File, the most recent year for which reliable (public use) income tax information is available.

The Public Use SOI is a stratified random sample of about 150,000 tax records representing the approximately 130 million federal income tax returns filed by individuals in the U.S. for tax year 2004. In order to assure the confidentiality of information contained on administrative tax returns, data items in the Public Use file are rounded and often masked, or blurred to prevent identification. As such, each individual tax record is only suggestive of an actual tax return filed. Each tax record contains detailed information of the income, deductions, exemptions, credits and tax payments of individuals and married couples. Stratification is done with respect to the size and composition of income, and high income taxpayers are over-sampled. This results in an analytical database which, though small in size, is accurate with respect to aggregate, economy- wide statistics.

For purposes of this study, the principal income items of interest in the data files are business income (and losses) received by sole proprietors and reported on Schedule C, partnership income and losses reported on Schedule E, and income or loss from Subchapter S corporations, also reported on Schedule E.[38] For sole proprietorships, which are the largest group of small businesses in the United States, the information available is quite detailed and includes net receipts, cost of goods sold, other income (e.g., interest received), depreciation, insurance, mortgage payments, other interest, office expenses, net wages and total deductions. For partnerships and S corporations, the information is more limited, but includes both active and passive income accruing to the business entity and the amount of the Section 179 deduction.[39]

The Quantria model supplements the available tax information in the Public Use File in several ways. First, because administrative tax data only become available with a significant lag due to tax filing deadlines, a proprietary extrapolation, or aging, module forecasts the microdata into future years. The extrapolation module relies on annual macroeconomic forecasts constructed by the Congressional Budget Office (CBO). CBO's forecasts of the macroeconomy are the official forecasts relied upon by congressional budget and tax analysts. Second, not all individuals or married couples are required to file federal income tax returns (e.g., their income may be below the filing threshold). The tax records in the Public Use File are therefore supplemented with additional information on non-filers identified from the Current Population Survey (CPS). The CPS is a monthly survey of labor force characteristics with an annual focus on income and demographics for the non-institutional population in the U.S.[40] Finally, the information on the input file is augmented with numerous imputations to support specialized tax policy analysis. As an example, many individuals receive their health insurance from employer-provided group insurance plans and the amount (if any) of the cost of this insurance that is paid by the employer is not taxable to the employee. Most economists argue, however, that this is a form of compensation and should be included in the taxpayers' income for purposes of classifying taxpayers. The Quantria microsimulation model includes an estimate of employer-provided health insurance premiums for each taxpayer.

## Identifying Small Businesses

Small business taxpayers are identified from individual tax records according to whether income is received in the form of sole proprietor income (Schedule C), partnership income (Schedule E), or S corporation income (Schedule E). It is not uncommon for certain taxpayers to have income from more than one business or in more than one form. This will affect the effective tax rate calculations in two ways. First, for a taxpayer who operates more than one business of the same entity type, information for each business is aggregated on the tax file across all businesses so an effective tax rate can only be calculated for all business income for each entity type. It can be argued that this is the correct conceptual framework from which to calculate effective tax rates for multiple businesses. In addition, this result has little, if any, effect on the effective tax rate calculations. Second, taxpayers with business income from more than one business-entity type are treated as separate businesses for purposes of the calculations. For example, a taxpayer who reports income from a sole proprietorship along with (active) income from an S corporation would be represented twice in the analysis. It can be argued that this is also the correct conceptual framework for examining small businesses.

## Calculating Effective Tax Rates

The Quantria microsimulation model calculates the effective tax rates of small business entities by running two simulations for each business entity type. In the first simulation (the "baseline" simulation), the total federal income tax liability is calculated for each taxpayer reporting net business income. In the second simulation (the "alternative scenario"), business income is removed from the calculation of tax liability, and the change in tax liability from the baseline case is measured. The net tax change (in this case, a tax reduction because income is reduced) is divided by net business income to calculate the effective tax rate. The following additional assumptions are made for each business entity type:

**Nonfarm sole proprietorships** – Small business nonfarm sole proprietorships are identified as those taxpayers who report net business receipts of less than $10 million on Schedule C. (The model excludes any taxpayer who reports net business income but reports no net business receipts.) In the alternative scenario, net business income is set to zero and federal income tax liability is recalculated.

**Partnerships and S Corporations** – A partnership or S corporation includes any taxpayer who reports net active income from partnerships or S corporations on Schedule E. For purposes of calculating net active income, 80 percent of the Section 179 deduction claimed is added back to account for the timing of depreciation deductions and to more closely approximate financial accounting conventions. Net non-passive income is used as a proxy for net receipts; thus, the analysis includes any taxpayer with less than $10 million in net active income. In the alternative scenario, net active income from total income (or loss) reported on Schedule E is subtracted and the difference in federal tax liability becomes the numerator in the effective tax rate calculations.

**C corporations** – The Quantria Strategies model cannot be used to calculate the effective tax rates of C corporations for two reasons. First, C corporations are subject to an entity-level tax (the corporate income tax). Second, no publicly available, micro level, federal income tax data is available for corporations, making it impossible to match individual level income taxes attributable to C corporation dividends and capital gains to specific C corporations. However, the IRS annually compiles tabulations of corporation information in its Corporate Source Book, which is an annual summary of the income, deductions, credits, taxes, and financial data (such as asset size) for all U.S. corporations. This summary data can be used to estimate the federal income tax liability and effective tax rate of small business C corporations.

## Industry Assignments

No information exists in the Public Use File that indicates the industry of the business where income is reported to have occurred. This is true of nonfarm sole proprietorships, partnerships and S corporations. This is in contrast to administrative data collected by the IRS from individual taxpayers who file Schedule C, for which NAICS industry codes are available. Industry codes are available on the primary business returns filed by small businesses (Form 1065 for partnerships; Form 1120-S for S corporations), but there is currently no publicly available information that connects tax returns filed by these pass-through entities with the owners of the business. As a result, it is not currently possible to directly link effective tax rates to specific industries through publicly available tax return data.

In order to approximate effective tax rates on an industry-by-industry basis, the Quantria Strategies Individual Income Tax Simulation Model imputes NAICS industry designation based on available, but very limited, information contained for each tax record. This imputation occurs in two steps: in the first step, an initial imputation is based on the reported net income of the business; in the second step, this imputation is calibrated based on aggregate reported income and losses reported by the IRS.

For nonfarm sole proprietorships, the initial imputation relies on the size of net business receipts to categorize businesses according to industry breakdowns contained in published IRS data. Once the size of receipts is known, businesses are randomly assigned to 11 industry groupings. A similar preliminary imputation is done for partnerships and S corporations. In the second stage of the imputation, these preliminary assignments are adjusted in an iterative manner to target IRS totals for net income and net losses by industry class.

Because of the significant data limitations, the industry-specific effective tax rate calculations contained in this study are only suggestive and are supported by very limited data. Nevertheless, the general trend of these calculations appears to align reasonably well with data reported in other studies. Refining the ability to calculate industry-specific effective tax rates should be a high priority area for future research.

## Limitations of This Analysis

The effective tax rate calculations in this study represent the first rigorous examination of the effective tax rates faced by small businesses in the United States. However, due to the nature in which federal income tax information is collected for different business types, there are several distinct limitations to this analysis. Because of the pass-through nature of partnerships and S corporations, actual income taxes paid only show up on the individual income tax returns of the owners of these businesses (i.e., partners in a partnership and shareholders of an S corporation), micro simulation is the only way to calculate the effect of federal income taxes on these businesses. Similarly, for nonfarm sole proprietorships, business income is commingled with income from other non-business sources, and isolating the taxes attributable to the business is difficult. Again, microsimulation seems the most reasonable and accurate way to measure the federal income taxes paid by these businesses.

In the case of small business C corporations, the effective tax rate calculations reflect only the entity level taxes (corporate income taxes) paid by the business. Although there are similarities between the individual and corporate income taxes, it must be noted that the effective tax rate calculation for C corporations is inherently different from the methodology used for pass-through entities and sole proprietorships.

The following additional points should be considered:

An explicit stacking order in the calculation of taxes attributable to the business is imposed by removing net business income last. This stacking order may result in a slightly higher estimate of tax liability for certain taxpayers because of the graduated rate structure.

Any multiple businesses owned by the same taxpayer are treated as separate entities. This methodology can, in some circumstances, result in different effective tax rates attributable to the same taxpayer for different businesses.

To the extent that some business owners (e.g., partners or S Corporation shareholders) are non-U.S. citizens or other entity types, then the income and taxes attributable to these entities is not counted.

The income of C corporations is taxed twice, once at the business level and once again when income is passed along to owners and investors, either as dividend payments or capital gain realizations. Because it is impossible to identify the tax payments by these owners, the calculations in this study underestimate the true effective tax burden of small business C corporations.

To the to the extent that small business owners receive a salary from the business – which may be the case for C Corporations – then there is no reliable way to identify those payments and calculate the income taxes paid on them from existing data. This will tend to understate the true tax liability of entities that provide compensation to their owners in this way.

# Appendix B. Federal Income Tax Provisions Applicable to Small Businesses

While the IRS uses a $10 million gross receipts threshold to identify small businesses for classification purposes, there is no single substantive definition of a small business that applies for federal tax purposes. Instead, the federal tax system often recognizes the unique circumstances of small businesses in specific industries by providing special rules that apply only to small businesses or to the owners of small business interests. How these special rules apply and what definition of small business is utilized depends upon the specific tax provision. In some cases, small businesses are subject to more onerous rules based on a perceived potential for abuse of the tax system.

This section provides a brief summary of the special income tax provisions identified in the federal tax code that are directly or indirectly applicable to small businesses. Because this paper explores federal income taxes only and does not examine the effects of other federal taxes, such as excise taxes, on small businesses, this section is limited to special income tax provisions affecting small businesses. It should be noted that there are also special provisions in the federal tax code that benefit small employers outside of the income tax area. For example, the special use valuation provisions (IRC sec. 2032A) applicable to farm and other real property may reduce the amount of estate taxes paid with respect to small businesses. Similarly, certain of the federal excise tax provisions have special rules for small businesses – see, for example, the exemption from federal firearms excise taxes for certain small manufacturers and the exemption from certain federal transportation excise taxes for small aircraft on nonestablished lines.

This summary generally is organized in ascending order by federal tax code provision. References to IRC sections are references to the Internal Revenue Code of 1986, as amended.

## 1. Graduated Individual and Corporate Tax Rates (IRC Secs. 1 and 11)

The graduated income tax rates for individuals and corporations have the effect of providing a lower marginal tax rate for many small businesses. Sole proprietors, partners of small partnerships, S corporation shareholders, and members of LLCs may all benefit from the graduated individual income tax rates (and the reduced rates of taxation on capital gains and dividends). Small corporations will benefit from the graduated corporate income tax rates.

## 2. Small Ethanol Producer Credit (IRC Sec. 40(b)(4))

In addition to the alcohol fuels credits generally provided under IRC section 40, small ethanol producers are provided a small ethanol producer credit of 10 cents per gallon of ethanol produced up to 15 million gallons in a year. A small ethanol producer is defined as a producer with a production capacity of up to 60 million gallons of alcohol per year.

## 3. Small Agri-biodiesel Producer Credit (IRC Sec. 40A(b)(5))

In addition to the credits for biodiesel and renewable diesel used as fuel generally provided under IRC section 40A, small agri-biodiesel producers are provided a small agri-biodiesel producer credit of 10 cents per gallon of qualified agri-biodiesel production up to 15 million gallons in a year. A small agri-biodiesel producer is defined as a producer with a production capacity of up to 60 million gallons of agri-biodiesel in a year.

## 4. Credit for Increasing Research Activities (IRC Sec. 41)

Taxpayers are generally entitled to claim a federal income tax credit for increasing research activities. Qualified research expenses include in-house research expenses and 65 percent of contract research expenses. A special provision permits a taxpayer to use 100 percent of contract research expenses for amounts paid to eligible small businesses. For this purpose, an eligible small business is a business in which the average number of employees during the preceding two calendar years was 500 or less.

While this provision does not provide a direct federal tax benefit to small businesses, it provides an incentive for other taxpayers to use eligible small businesses for qualified contract research activities.

## 5. Credit for Expenditures to Provide Access to Disabled Individuals (IRC Sec. 44)

Eligible small businesses are entitled to claim a credit for 50 percent of the expenditures incurred during a year to make a business accessible to the disabled. The expenditures eligible for the credit are those in excess of $250 and less than $10,250. Thus, the maximum credit is 50 percent of $10,000 ($10,250-$250) or $5,000.

An eligible small business for purposes of the credit is any taxpayer that either (1) had gross receipts (less returns and allowances) for the preceding taxable year that did not exceed $1 million or (2) had no more than 30 full-time employees during the preceding taxable year.[41]

## 6. Credit for Electricity Produced from Certain Renewable Resources (IRC Sec. 45)

The credit for electricity produced from certain renewable resources is available to qualified energy resources, which includes small irrigation power. For purposes of this credit, small irrigation power is defined as power generated without any dam or impoundment of water through an irrigation system canal or ditch and whose capacity rating is more than 149 kilowatts, but less than 5 megawatts.

## 7. Credit for Portion of Employer Social Security Taxes Paid with Respect to Employee Cash Tips (IRC Sec. 45B)

An employer in the food and beverage industry is entitled to claim a credit against federal taxes for its portion of social security and Medicare taxes (FICA taxes) paid on employee tips. While this provision is not specifically applicable to small businesses, many food and beverage establishments qualifying for the credit are likely to be small businesses.

## 8. Credit for Small Employer Pension Plan Startup Costs (IRC Sec. 45E)

Small employers are entitled to claim a credit for 50 percent of their qualified startup costs for establishing a retirement plan for their employees. The amount of the credit cannot exceed $500 per year for up to three years. A small employer eligible for the credit is defined as an employer that had no more than 100 employees who received at least $5,000 in compensation for the preceding year.

## 9. Credit for Production of Low-sulfur Diesel Fuel (IRC Sec. 45H)

Qualified small business refiners are entitled to a credit for qualified expenditures for the production of low-sulfur diesel fuel. A small business refiner for this purpose is defined as a refiner of crude oil that employs no more than 1,500 individuals on any day during the year and had an average daily refinery production during the one-year period ending on December 31, 2002, which did not exceed 205,000 barrels.

## 10. Alternative Minimum Tax (IRC Sec. 55)

Small corporations are exempt from the corporate alternative minimum tax. Small corporations are defined as those corporations that have average annual gross receipts of no more than $7.5 million for all 3-year periods ending before the taxable year ($5 million for the first 3-year period).

## 11. Election to Expense Certain Depreciable Business Assets (IRC Sec. 179)

Businesses are allowed to take a current deduction (expense) for the cost of certain property rather than take a depreciation deduction each year over the life of the property. The expensing deduction is only available for up to $250,000 (for 2008) of qualifying expenses and is phased out dollar for dollar if the total amount of such property purchased during the year exceeds $800,000 (for 2008). Although not specifically limited to small businesses, section 179 expensing tends to benefit small businesses.

## 12. Treatment of Certain Qualified Film and Television Production (IRC Sec. 181)

Expensing is allowed for the cost of any qualified film or television production if the aggregate cost does not exceed $15 million ($20 million in the case of production in certain areas). While not directly limited to small businesses, this provision has the effect of benefiting smaller film and television producers. The provision expires after 2008.

## 13. Start-up Expenditures (IRC Sec. 195) and Corporation Organizational Expenses (IRC Sec. 248)

In general, taxpayers cannot deduct currently the start-up expenditures for a new business. Instead, these start-up expenses are amortized over a period of at least 180 months, starting with the month in which the business begins. However, taxpayers can elect to deduct up to $5,000 for start-up expenditures for a new business (sec. 195). The $5,000 amount is phased out for each dollar of start-up expenditures in excess of $50,000. This provision has the effect of benefiting new small businesses. A similar provision applies with respect to the organizational expenditures for a new corporation (sec. 248).

## 14. Archer MSAs (IRC Sec. 220)

Self-employed individuals and employees of small businesses are permitted to deduct contributions to an Archer medical savings account (MSA). A small employer for this purpose means an employer with an average of 50 or fewer employees during either of the two preceding calendar years. No new deductible contributions are permitted to Archer MSAs after 2007 unless the individual previously had an MSA or works for an employer that made MSA contributions.

## 15. Golden Parachute Payments (IRC Sec. 280G)

No deduction is allowed for any excess parachute payment, which is a payment in the nature of a severance payment made to a former executive of a business after he or she leaves the business. There is an exception for payments made to an individual from a small business corporation which could qualify for S corporation treatment (generally has no more than 100 shareholders who are all individuals, estates, trust, and certain other entities). (See sec. 1361(b) and the discussion in Part V for a description of the requirements for S corporation treatment.)

## 16. SIMPLE Retirement Accounts (IRC Sec. 408(p))

Small employers are entitled to adopt a simplified qualified retirement plan for their employees, called SIMPLE retirement accounts. These plans have fewer rules and restrictions than the rules that normally apply to employer-sponsored qualified retirement plans.

For purposes of the SIMPLE retirement accounts, a small employer is defined as an employer that had no more than 100 employees who received at least $5,000 in compensation for the preceding year.

## 17. Special Rules for Top-heavy Plans (IRC Sec. 416)

Employer retirement plans that are top heavy are required to meet additional requirements, including providing minimum contributions on behalf of employees, which increases the cost of the retirement plan for the employer. An employer retirement plan is top heavy if more than 60 percent of the benefits or account balances under the plan benefit key employees. Key employees are certain owners and officers of the business. Although the top heavy rules do not specifically apply to small businesses, the rules are most likely to apply to such businesses.

## 18. Method of Accounting for Corporations Engaged in Farming (IRC Sec. 447)

Corporations and partnerships that have a corporate partner engaged in farming generally are required to use the accrual method of accounting. However, an exception to this rule provides that an S corporation and a C corporation with gross receipts that do not exceed $1 million in the taxable year are not required to use the accrual method of accounting. In the case of family corporations, the gross receipts threshold is increased to $25,000.

## 19. Limitation on Use of Cash Method of Accounting (IRC Sec. 448)

Certain taxpayers (C corporations, partnerships with a C corporation partner, and tax shelters) are not permitted to use the cash method of accounting. An exception applies for farming businesses, and qualified personal service corporations, and corporations or partnerships with average annual gross receipts of no more than $5 million for the three taxable years prior to the current year. A qualified personal service corporation is engaged substantially in the performance of service in the fields of health, law, engineering, architecture, accounting, actuarial science, performing arts, or consulting.

## 20. Simplified Dollar-value LIFO Method for Certain Small Businesses (IRC Sec. 474)

An eligible small business may elect to use a simplified dollar-value method for pricing inventories. An eligible small business for this purpose must have annual average gross receipts for the three preceding taxable years of not more than $5 million.

## 21. Exemption from Federal Income Tax for Small Life Insurance Companies (IRC Sec. 501(c)(15))

Certain small life insurance companies are exempt from federal income tax. A small life insurance company is a life insurance company (1) with gross receipts for the taxable year that do not exceed $600,000 and more than 50 percent of the gross receipts consist of premiums or (2) is a mutual insurance company with gross receipts for the taxable year that do not exceed $150,000 and more than 35 percent of the gross receipts consist of premiums.

## 22. Small Life Insurance Company Deduction (IRC Sec. 806)

A small life insurance company is permitted a deduction equal to 60 percent of the company's tentative life insurance company taxable income (LICTI) up to $3 million. The deduction is phased out for tentative LICTI between $3 million and $15 million. In addition, the small life insurance company deduction is disallowed if a company has assets of $500 million or more.

## 23. Alternative Tax for Certain Small Nonlife Insurance Companies (IRC Sec. 831(b))

In lieu of the normal corporate income tax rate structure, small property and casualty insurance companies are subject to tax only on their investment income. This provision applies to insurance companies other than life insurance companies if the net written premiums (or, if greater, direct written premiums) for the taxable year do not exceed $1.2 million.

## 24. Rollover of Gain from Qualified Small Business Stock to Another Qualified Small Business Stock (IRC Sec. 1045)

Taxpayers can avoid paying taxes on gain from the sale of qualified small business stock (as defined by sec. 1202 (see item 25, below)) by rolling over the gain to other qualified small business stock within 60 days of the sale.

## 25. Exclusion of Capital Gain from Small Business Stock (IRC Sec. 1202)

An individual taxpayer can exclude up to 50 percent (60 percent if the qualified small business stock was issued by a small business in an empowerment zone) of the gain from the sale or exchange of qualified small business stock held for more than five years. There is a cumulative limit on the exclusion of the greater of $10 million or 10 times the taxpayer's adjusted basis of all qualified stock the issuer disposed of during the taxable year.

For purposes of this exclusion, qualified small business stock must have been issued after August 10, 1993, and the issuing corporation must be a domestic C corporation with aggregate gross assets that do not exceed $50 million as of the date of issuance. At least 80 percent of the value of the corporation's assets must be used in the active conduct of one or more qualified trades or businesses. Qualified trades or businesses do not include health, law, engineering, architecture, hospitality, farming, insurance, financing, or mineral extraction, but SSBICs qualify. (SSBICs are discussed in the following section).

## 26. Small Business Investment Companies (IRC Secs. 243(a)(2), 1242, 1243, and 1044)

A small business investment company (SBIC) is a private corporation operating under the Small Business Investment Act of 1958. SBICs provide capital to small businesses through the purchase of convertible debentures. An SBIC is entitled to special treatment under certain circumstances: First, an SBIC is entitled to a 100 percent dividends received deduction (rather than 70 percent) for the dividends received from taxable domestic corporations (sec. 243(a)(2)). In addition, an SBIC may treat as an ordinary (rather than capital) loss any loss from the sale or exchange of the stock of a small business under certain conditions (sec. 1243) and any loss on the sale of SBIC stock (or if the stock becomes worthless) (sec. 1242).

In addition, individuals and C corporations can defer recognition of capital gains on the sale of publicly traded securities if they use the sale proceeds within 60 days to purchase common stock or a partnership interest in a specialized small business investment company (SSBIC). An individual can defer up to $50,000 per year and $500,000 total; C corporations can defer up to $250,000 per year and $1 million total.

## 27. Losses on Small Business Stock (IRC Sec. 1244)

Individuals are allowed to take an ordinary loss deduction for losses on the sale, exchange, or worthlessness of small business stock. The maximum amount deductible in any year is $50,000 for a single individual and $100,000 for a married couple. The stock must have been issued to the individual (or a partner in a partnership) in exchange for money or property other than stock or securities.

For purposes of this provision, a small business corporation is a corporation with respect to which, at the time the stock was issued, the aggregate amount of money and other property received by the corporation as a contribution to capital and as paid-in surplus did not exceed $1 million and for the corporation's five most recent taxable years, more than 50 percent of its gross receipts were derived from sources other than royalties, rents, dividends, interest, annuities, and gains from the sale of securities. In other words, the corporation must be conducting active, rather than passive, activities.

## 28. Averaging of Farm Income (IRC Sec. 1301)

Individuals engaged in a farming business can elect to average their income over three years for federal income tax purposes.

## 29. S Corporations (IRC Sec. 1361)

A small business corporation (S corporation) can elect to be treated as a pass-through entity, rather than a corporation, for federal tax purposes. To be eligible for S corporation status, a small business corporation must (1) be a domestic corporation; (2) have no more than 100 shareholders; (3) have shareholders that are only individuals, estates, certain tax-exempt organizations, and certain trusts; (4) have no nonresident alien shareholders; (5) have only one class of stock; (6) not be a bank, insurance company, possessions corporation, or a domestic international sales corporation; and (7) meet certain other requirements.

## End Notes

[1] This study does not explore the effects of other federal taxes on small businesses, such as excise taxes, the payroll tax system, and estate and gift taxes. Theoretically, the research in this study could be expanded in the future to examine all federal taxes.

[2] Based on the imputations from the Quantria Strategies, LLC Individual Income Tax Model using the 2004 IRS Statistics of Income Individual Income Tax Public Use File and tabulations of selected cell-based data on the net income and taxes of C corporations from the IRS 2004 Corporation Source Book. The Individual Income Tax Public Use File captures the federal income taxes attributable to business activities of sole proprietors, partnerships, and S corporations, while the Corporation Source Book permits an approximation of the federal income taxes of C corporations.

[3] C corporations are permitted a current deduction for amounts paid as reasonable compensation to shareholders who are also employees of the corporation.

[4] Appendix B provides a listing of these special tax provisions.

[5] This study does not explore the effects of other federal taxes on small businesses, such as excise taxes, the payroll tax system, and estate and gift taxes. Theoretically, the research in this study could be expanded in the future to examine all federal taxes.

[6] In addition, in the case of small corporations, the owner of the business may attempt to withdraw business profits in the form of compensation for his or her services for the business. Corporations are allowed to deduct their ordinary and necessary business expenses, which include compensation expenses, from their gross income. Thus, reasonable compensation paid by a corporation reduces the taxable income subject to the federal corporate income tax. While there are rules that are intended to prevent owners of small corporations from receiving "unreasonable compensation" as a way of avoiding corporate income taxes, the determination of what constitutes unreasonable compensation can be difficult to make and more difficult to police. This study does not attempt to measure the extent to which corporate profits are paid and taxed to a small business owner as compensation for services.

[7] Appendix B contains a list of the special small business provisions contained in the Internal Revenue Code of 1986.

[8] The most recent publicly available data on the IRS Statistics of Income website generally is 2005. However, the most recent publicly available micro (or firm or entity level) data is 2004. In order to be consistent with the micro data, the 2004 aggregate data is used in this section.

[9] We will point out at the outset that the rates computed for C corporations in this analysis are not comparable to those borne by other forms of organization. This is due to two key factors: first, existing data do not allow taxes on salary payments to be traced to the owners; and second, the data also do not allow the capture of taxes paid on corporate income distributed to shareholders in the forms of dividends and capital gains.

[10] A single person LLC whose sole owner is an individual files an individual income tax return with Schedule C, E, or F. A single person LLC whose sole owner is a corporation includes its income and expenses on the corporation's tax return.

[11] Approximately 450,000 of these returns were sole proprietorships registered as LLCs.

[12] There was a substantial (20 percent) increase in the deductions claimed for car and truck expenses from 2004 to 2005. This increase could be partly attributable to increases in fuel costs.

[13] S corporation returns with receipts under $10 million comprised nearly 70 percent of total S corporation receipts.

[14] The greater proportion of interest expenses for C corporations may represent the prevalence of debt financing.

[15] *U.S. Multinational Corporations. Effective Tax Rates Are Correlated with Where Income is Reported.* United States General Accountability Office, GAO-08-950, August 2008.

[16] Beginning in 2004, the IRS required most large corporations to complete a new schedule (M-3) as part of its filing requirements. In addition to reconciling reported differences between financial (i.e., book) and tax accounting measures, the new schedule requires the company to show domestic and foreign-source income separately.

[17] *Tax Policy. 1989 and 1989 Company Effective Tax Rates Higher Than in Previous Years.* U.S. General Accounting Office, GAO.GGD-92-111, August 2002.

[18] *The Impact of Tax Expenditure Policies on Incorporated Small Businesses.* Innovation & Information Consultants, Inc. U.S. Small Business Administration, Office of Advocacy, 2004. www.sba.gov/advo/research/rs237tot.pdf.

[19] McIntyre, Robert S. and Nguyen, T.D. Coo. *Corporate Income Taxes in the Bush Years.* A Joint Project of Citizens for Tax Justice and the Institute on Taxation and Economic Policy, September *2004. www.ctj.org/corpfed04an.pdf.* McIntyre, Robert S. and Nguyen, T.D. Coo. *Corporate Income Taxes in the 1990's.* Institute on Taxation and Economic Policy, October 2000. http://www.itepnet.org/corp00an.pdf.

[20] Estimates of state and local income taxes incurred are subtracted from net income.

[21] *Historical Effective Federal Tax Rates: 1979 to 2005.* Congressional Budget Office, December 2007.

[22] "Taxing Capital Income: Effective Rates and Approaches to Reform." Congressional Budget Office, October 2005. Gravelle, Jane G. "Capital Income Tax Revisions and Effective Tax Rates." Congressional Research Office Report for Congress, October 2, 2003.

[23] See Appendix B for a review of the specific small business provisions contained in the Internal Revenue Code.

[24] A separate rule denies a deduction for certain compensation in excess of $1 million paid to employees by publicly held corporations, but this rule is unlikely to apply to most small businesses.

[25] The AMT exemption amount for married couples is $45,000, but a temporary increase in the exemption amount has been passed by the Congress each year to increase the exemption amount and reduce the number of people subject to the AMT. For 2008, the exemption amount for a married couple filing a joint return is $69,950.

[26] *Private Health Insurance. Small Employers Continue to Face Challenges in Providing Coverage.* A Report to the Ranking Minority Member, Committee on Small Business and Entrepreneurship, U.S. Senate. U.S. General Accountability Office. GAO-02-8, October 2001.

[27] Examples of the types of retirement savings plans an employer could establish include defined benefit plans, defined contribution plans, 401(k) plans, cash balance plans, and SIMPLE plans. Defined benefit plans promise a specific benefit at retirement age; employers are required to satisfy complex funding rules and need to use the services of an actuary. Under defined contribution plans, including 401(k) plans, employees are entitled to an account balance, rather than a specific benefit. SIMPLE plans are designed to provide a simplified retirement savings arrangement for small employers.

[28] There are some situations where S corporations may incur some federal income tax liability, but they are not germane to this study.

[29] Sample weights are used to calculate aggregate, economy-wide totals.

[30] As explained above, any taxpayer that reports more than $10 million in net business receipts from any business entity is excluded.

[31] There is an implicit "stacking order" underlying this calculation. In effect, business income is assumed to be taxed last after all other non-business sources of income have been taxed. This convention will have the effect of slightly overstating the true effective tax rate in some circumstances.

[32] Actually, the absolute value of the change in tax liability is used, since according to the methodology used, this would result in a reduction in total taxes when income is reduced.

[33] This would happen, for example, if the taxpayer operated a sole proprietorship and also was a partner in a partnership.

[34] This is expected to have a negligible effect on the calculations. Most partnerships, for example, are comprised of individuals.

[35] Appendix B provides a listing of these special tax provisions.

[36] This is consistent with most prior studies that measure effective tax rates.

[37] As a result, the total number of C corporations in these tables (classified by size of assets) differs somewhat from those numbers reported earlier in this report where small businesses are classified according to the size of business receipts.

[38] As mentioned in the body of the report, certain types of business income received by C corporations may show up on tax returns as wage income or capital gains (or losses). The source of these income payments cannot be identified in the Public Use File.

[39] More information on the Public Use File can be found in "General Description Booklet for the 2004 Public Use Tax File," Individual Statistics Branch, Statistics of Income Division, Internal Revenue Service, September, 2007.

[40] The March CPS includes questions relating to income and employment that are asked retrospectively to the prior year. For purposes of this study, the CPS information for non-filers is obtained from the March 2005 survey to align with the 2004 tax year data in the Public Use File.

[41] Full-time employees are defined as those who work at least 30 hours per week for at least 20 calendar weeks during the taxable year.

In: Small Business Tax Issues and Benefits ISBN: 978-1-61668-806-6
Editors: Alton E. Kastenberg © 2010 Nova Science Publishers, Inc.

*Chapter 2*

# SMALL BUSINESS EXPENSING ALLOWANCE: CURRENT STATUS, LEGISLATIVE PROPOSALS, AND ECONOMIC EFFECTS

***Gary Guenther***

## SUMMARY

Under the American Recovery and Reinvestment Act of 2009 (ARRA, P.L. 111-5), business taxpayers may expense (or deduct as a current expense) up to $250,000 of the total cost of certain depreciable assets placed in service in 2009, within certain limits. One limit is a phaseout threshold, which is set at $800,000 in 2009. The act also allows business taxpayers to claim a so- called bonus depreciation allowance in 2009 that is equal to 50% of the cost of qualified assets placed in service that year. Firms unable to use either option for accelerated depreciation have to write off that cost over a longer period, using current depreciation schedules. The rules governing the use of the allowance confine most of its benefits to relatively small firms.

This report focuses on the economic effects of what is referred to as the small business expensing allowance. It begins by explaining how the allowance works, then summarizes its legislative history and describes legislation in the 111$^{th}$ Congress to modify the allowance, and concludes with a discussion of the allowance's implications for economic efficiency, equity, and tax administration. The report will be updated as necessary.

There was strong bipartisan support for enhancing the expensing allowance in recent Congresses, and there are some early signs that this support has not waned in the 111th Congress. Several bills to extend the enhanced allowance that was in effect in 2008 through 2009 or 2010 have been introduced, capped by H.R. 1, the American Recovery and Reinvestment Act of 2009. The version of H.R. 1 signed by President Obama contains a provision that would allow firms to claim the same enhanced expensing allowance in 2009 that was available in 2008. The act also extends through 2009 the 50% bonus depreciation allowance that applied to the purchase of qualified assets in 2008.

The expensing allowance appears to have a minor effect on the composition and allocation of business investment, the distribution of the federal tax burden among income groups, and the cost of tax compliance for smaller firms. These effects correspond to the three traditional criteria for evaluating tax policy: efficiency, equity, and simplicity. While the allowance has the potential to spur increased small business investment by reducing the user cost of capital and increasing the cash flow of firms that use the allowance, it can also harm economic efficiency by encouraging greater investment in activities with relatively low pre-tax rates of return. At the same time, the allowance appears to have no measurable impact on the distribution of the federal tax burden among income groups, but it simplifies tax accounting for firms claiming it.

Provided certain conditions are met, firms may expense (or deduct as a current expense) up to $250,000 of the total cost of qualified assets they purchase and place in service in 2009. Some refer to this option for capital cost recovery as the small business expensing allowance, as the rules governing its use confine the allowance's benefits mainly to firms that are relatively small in asset, employment, or revenue size. Generally, firms that cannot use the expensing allowance may recover the cost of the same assets over longer periods by claiming allowable depreciation deductions. The expensing allowance represents a significant tax subsidy for small business investment, as it reduces the marginal effective rate at which the returns to investment in qualified assets are taxed.

The 111th Congress has already passed a bill (H.R. 1, the American Recovery and Reinvestment Act of 2009 or ARRA, P.L. 111-5) that extends through 2009 an enhanced version of the allowance that was available in 2008. It is hoped that such an investment tax subsidy will spur many small firms to spend more on new equipment in 2009 than they otherwise would.

This report examines the current status of the small business expensing allowance, initiatives in the 111th Congress to modify it, and its main economic effects The report begins by describing the allowance's design and summarizing its legislative history. It then discusses proposals in the current Congress to modify the current allowance. The report concludes with an assessment of the allowance's implications for economic efficiency, equity, and tax administration.

# CURRENT EXPENSING ALLOWANCE

Under section 179 of the Internal Revenue Code (IRC), firms in all lines of business have the option of expensing the cost of qualified assets (or property) they acquire in the year when the assets are placed in service, within certain limits. In general, business taxpayers that are unable or unwilling to take advantage of the expensing allowance may recover this cost over longer periods by using allowable depreciation deductions.

## Maximum Expensing Allowance

The maximum expensing allowance is $250,000 for qualified assets placed in service in 2009 by firms located outside so-called enterprise and empowerment zones (EZs), renewal communities (RCs), and presidentially declared disaster areas (PDDAs).[1] (For the sake of clarity, this allowance is henceforth referred to as the regular allowance.) For firms operating within all special areas except PDDAs, the maximum allowance for qualified assets placed in service in 2009 is $285,000. For firms located in PDDAs, the maximum allowance for qualified assets placed in service in 2009 is $350,000.

In 2010, the regular allowance is scheduled to drop to $125,000, before adjustment for inflation; it will be $160,000 for firms located in special areas other than PDDAs, and $225,000 for PDDA firms; both amounts are indexed for inflation. Assuming no change in current law, the regular allowance is scheduled in 2011 and beyond to drop to $25,000, its amount before the enactment of the Jobs and Growth Tax Relief Reconciliation Act of 2003 (JGTRRA), with no adjustment for inflation. Beginning in 2011, the allowance will fall to $60,000 for firms operating in all special areas except PDDAs.

## Qualified Property

Qualified property is defined as certain new and used depreciable assets—as specified in IRC Section 1245(a)(3)—acquired for use in the active conduct of a trade or business. With a few exceptions, this property consists of business machines and equipment used in connection with manufacturing or production, extraction, transportation, communications, electricity, gas, water, and sewage disposal. Transportation equipment with an unloaded gross weight of more than 6,000 pounds (including heavy-duty sport utility vehicles) is considered qualified property, but not heating and air conditioning units. In addition, the cost of packaged computer software acquired for business use may be expensed through 2009. Most buildings and their structural components do not qualify for the regular allowance, but research and bulk storage facilities do qualify.

The expensing allowance does not apply to qualified property placed in service in the following kinds of establishments located in EZs, RCs, and PDDAs: private or commercial golf courses, country clubs, massage parlors, hot-tub and suntan facilities, stores whose principal business is the sale of alcoholic beverages, racetracks, and facilities used for gambling.

## Limitations on the Use of the Expensing Allowance

The maximum amount of qualified property that may be expensed in a single tax year under IRC Section 179 is subject to two explicit limitations: a dollar limitation and an income limitation.

Under the dollar limitation, the regular expensing allowance is reduced, dollar for dollar, by the amount by which the total cost of qualified property placed in service during the year exceeds a phaseout threshold. For firms operating in EZs, RCs, and the NYLZ, the expensing allowance is reduced by half of the amount by which the total cost of qualified property placed in service in a tax year exceeds the threshold. The threshold is set at $800,000 in 2009 for all firms except those operating in PDDAs, which face a threshold of $1,400,000.[2] As a result, a business taxpayer located outside the special areas may expense none of the cost of qualified property it places in service in 2009 when the total cost equals or exceeds $1,050,000. This means, for example, that if such a firm were to place in service in 2009 qualified property whose total cost came to $550,000, it could deduct the entire amount under IRC Section 179.

The phaseout threshold for the regular allowance is scheduled to fall to \$500,000 in 2010, with an adjustment for inflation. Assuming no change in current law, the threshold is scheduled to revert to its pre-JGTRRA level of \$200,000 (with no indexation for inflation) in 2011 and beyond.

Under the income limitation, the expensing allowance a firm claims cannot exceed its taxable income (including wages and salaries) from the active conduct of the trade or business in which the qualified assets are employed. For example, if the firm in the above example were to have taxable income in 2009 of \$25,000 from the business in which the qualified property is used, it would be able to claim an expensing allowance of no more than \$25,000. While business taxpayers are not allowed to carry forward any expensing allowance lost because of the dollar limitation, they may carry forward indefinitely any allowance denied because of the income limitation.

Business taxpayers can also expect to face a new restriction on their ability to take advantage of the expensing option in 2011. Under Internal Revenue Service (IRS) Regulation 1.179-5, taxpayers currently may make or revoke an election under IRC Section 179 for property placed in service through 2010 without the consent of the IRS Commissioner by submitting an amended tax return for the tax year in question. For tax years beginning in 2011, however, an expensing election may be revoked only with the consent of the Commissioner.

## Bonus Depreciation Allowance

In addition to the expensing allowance, business taxpayers were able to claim a temporary 30% first-year depreciation deduction under the Job Creation and Worker Assistance Act of 2002 (P.L. 107-147), or a temporary 50% first-year depreciation deduction under Jobs and Growth Tax Relief Reconciliation Act of 2003 (JGTRRA, P.L. 108-26). Both deductions were commonly referred to as bonus depreciation allowances and operated as partial expensing allowances. They applied to new (but not used) property eligible for depreciation under the modified accelerated cost recovery system (MACRS) and having a depreciation life of less than 20 years. Qualified property acquired between September 11, 2001 and December 31, 2004, and placed in service before January 1, 2005, was eligible for the 30% depreciation deduction. The 50% deduction applied to qualified property bought between May 6, 2003 and January 1, 2005, and placed in service by January 1, 2006. Since there was an overlap of nearly 19 months between the two options for accelerated depreciation, business taxpayers were allowed to claim only one of them.

The Economic Stimulus Act of 2008 (P.L. 110-185) reinstated the 50% first-year bonus depreciation allowance that expired at the end of 2006. It applies to the same set of depreciable assets targeted by the earlier deduction. To benefit from this allowance, a firm had to buy qualified assets and place them in service between January 1, 2008, and December 31, 2008; an exception was made for assets with relatively long production schedules, such as aircraft. The allowance expired at the end of 2008.

As a result of the ARRA, the bonus depreciation allowance that was available in 2008 has been extended through 2009.

For property that is eligible for both the expensing and special depreciation allowances, a firm is required to write off the property's cost in a prescribed order. The expensing allowance must be taken first, an act that reduces a taxpayer's basis in the property by the amount of the allowance. Then the taxpayer may apply the 50% first-year bonus depreciation allowance to any remaining basis, further reducing the taxpayer's basis in the property. Finally, the taxpayer is allowed to claim a depreciation allowance under the MACRS on any remaining basis, using the double declining balance method. Firms using all three allowances realize a significant reduction in their cost of capital for investment in qualified property, as will be discussed below in some detail.

## LEGISLATIVE HISTORY OF THE EXPENSING ALLOWANCE

The expensing allowance under IRC Section 179 originated as a special first-year depreciation allowance that was included in the Small Business Tax Revision Act of 1958 (P.L. 85-866). It was intended to reduce the tax burden on small business owners, stimulate small business investment, and simplify tax accounting for smaller firms. The deduction was limited to $2,000 (or $4,000 in the case of a married couple filing a joint return) of the cost of new and used business machines and equipment with a depreciation life of six or more years.

This allowance remained in effect until the passage of the Economic Recovery Tax Act of 1981 (ERTA, P.L. 97-34). ERTA replaced the special deduction with a maximum expensing allowance of $5,000 and laid down a timetable for gradually increasing the allowance to $10,000 by 1986. Despite these enhancements, few firms took advantage of the new allowance. Some analysts ascribed the tepid response to the limitations on the use of the investment tax credit that was also established by ERTA. A business taxpayer claiming the credit for the acquisition of an asset that also was eligible for the expensing allowance could claim the credit only for the portion of the cost that was not expensed; so the full credit could be used only if no expensing allowance was claimed. For many firms, the tax savings from the credit only evidently outweighed the tax savings from a combination of the credit and the allowance.

In a bid to counter the growing federal budget deficits of the early 1980s, Congress passed the Deficit Reduction Act of 1984 (P.L. 98-369). One of its provisions postponed from 1986 to 1990 the scheduled increase in the maximum expensing allowance to $10,000. Use of the allowance rose markedly following the repeal of the investment tax credit by the Tax Reform Act of 1986.

The maximum allowance reached $10,000 in 1990, as scheduled, and remained at that amount until the passage of the Omnibus Budget Reconciliation Act of 1993 (OBRA93, P.L. 103-66). OBRA93 raised the maximum allowance to $17,500 (as of January 1, 1993) and added a variety of tax benefits for special areas known as enterprise zones and empowerment zones. One of these benefits was an expensing allowance for qualified assets placed in service in an EZ that was $20,000 greater than the regular allowance, with a phaseout threshold twice as large as the phaseout threshold for the regular allowance. To be designated as an EZ, an area had to meet a variety of eligibility criteria relating to population, poverty rate, and geographic size.

With the passage of the Small Business Job Protection Act of 1996 (P.L. 104-188), the regular allowance embarked on yet another upward path. The act raised the maximum allowance to $18,000 in 1997, $18,500 in 1998, $19,000 in 1999, $20,000 in 2000, $24,000 in 2001 and 2002, and $25,000 in 2003 and thereafter.

Under the Community Renewal Tax Relief Act of 2000 (P.L. 106-544), Congress expanded the list of special areas to include renewal communities and granted them the same tax benefits available to EZs, including an enhanced expensing allowance. The act also increased the maximum allowance for qualified assets placed in service in a tax year in all special areas (including RCs) to $35,000 above the regular allowance.

In response to the economic effects of the terrorist attacks of September 11, 2001, Congress established a variety of tax benefits through the Job Creation and Worker Assistance Act of 2002 (P.L. 107-147) to encourage new business investment in the section of lower Manhattan in New York City that bore the brunt of the attacks on the World Trade Center. The act designated this area as the New York "Liberty Zone." Among the tax benefits offered to firms investing in the zone was the same enhanced expensing allowance available for qualified investments in EZs and RCs.

The regular allowance remained on the upward path set down by the Small Business Jobs Protection Act until the adoption of JGTRRA. Under JGTRRA, the maximum regular allowance rose four-fold to $100,000 as of May 6, 2003 and was supposed to stay at that amount in 2004 and 2005, before returning to its amount before the enactment of JGTRRA ($25,000) in 2006 and thereafter. JGTRRA also raised the phaseout threshold to $400,000 over the same period, indexed both the regular allowance and the threshold for inflation in 2004 and 2005, and added off-theshelf software for business use to the list of depreciable assets eligible for expensing from May 6, 2003 through December 31, 2005.

The American Jobs Creation Act of 2004 (AJCA, P.L. 108-357) extended the changes in the allowance made by JGTRRA through the end of 2007.

In an effort to spur economic recovery in the areas of Louisiana, Mississippi, and Alabama devastated by Hurricane Katrina, Congress passed the Gulf Opportunity Zone Act of 2005 (P.L. 109-135). Among other things, the act designated these areas as the Gulf Opportunity Zone (GOZ) and offered a variety of tax incentives for new business investment in the GOZ, including an enhanced expensing allowance for qualified assets purchased on or after August 28, 2005, and placed in service by December 31, 2007. This allowance could be as much as $100,000 above the regular allowance. In addition, it began to phase out when the total cost of qualified assets placed in service in a tax year exceeded a threshold that was $600,000 above the phaseout threshold for the regular allowance. Finally, more assets were eligible for the enhanced allowance than for the regular allowance.

The Tax Increase Prevention and Reconciliation Act of 2005 (P.L. 109-222) extended the changes in the allowance made by JGTRRA through 2009.

Under the U.S. Troop Readiness, Veterans' Care, Katrina Recovery, and Iraq Appropriations Act, 2007 (P.L. 110-28), Congress extended the changes in the allowance made by JGTRRA yet again (through 2010), raised the maximum allowance to $125,000 and the phaseout threshold to $500,000 from 2007 through 2010, and indexed both amounts for inflation from 2008 through 2010. The act also extended through 2008 the enhanced expensing allowance for qualified assets placed in service in the GOZ.

In a bid to boost business investment in the midst of an accelerating downturn in economic activity, Congress increased the allowance to $250,000 and the phaseout threshold to $800,000 for 2008 only through the Economic Stimulus Act of 2008 (P.L. 110-185). Those amounts return to $125,000 and $500,000 (both amounts adjusted for inflation) in 2009 and 2010.

The American Recovery and Reinvestment Act of 2009 (P.L. 111-5) extended the enhanced allowance created by the Economic Stimulus Act of 2008 through 2009.

## LEGISLATIVE INITIATIVES IN THE 111TH CONGRESS

There are some early signs that congressional interest in enhancing the expensing allowance to boost small business investment remains as robust as ever in the 111th Congress. Several bills to extend through 2009 or 2010 the enhanced allowance that was available in 2008 have been introduced, capped by H.R. 1(ARRA, P.L. 111-5). The version of H.R. 1 signed by President Obama contains a provision that allows firms to claim a maximum expensing allowance of $250,000, with a phaseout threshold of $800,000, for qualified assets placed in service in 2009. The act also extends through 2009 the 50-percent bonus depreciation allowance that applied to the purchase of qualified assets in 2008.

## ECONOMIC EFFECTS OF THE EXPENSING ALLOWANCE

For many lawmakers, the expensing allowance represents a desirable policy tool for lowering the tax burden on small business owners and stimulating business investment at the same time. And for many small business owners, the allowance represents a desirable tax benefit. But for most public finance economists, the allowance generates economic effects that go beyond its impact on the tax burden of small business owners. In their view, the allowance could affect the allocation of investment capital within the private sector, the distribution of the federal tax burden among major income groups, and the cost of tax compliance for smaller firms. These effects correspond to the three traditional criteria for evaluating tax policy: efficiency, equity, and simplicity. Each is discussed below.

## Efficiency Effects

Efficiency lies at the heart of traditional economic theory and analysis. It refers to the allocation of resources in an economy and how that allocation shapes the welfare of consumers and producers. When the allocation of resources produces the greatest possible economic surplus— defined as the total value to buyers of the goods and services they consume minus the total cost to sellers of providing these goods and services—the allocation is said to be efficient. But when the allocation is less than efficient, some of the possible gains from exchange among buyers and sellers are not realized. For example, economists deem an allocation of resources inefficient when most suppliers of a good fail to produce it at the lowest marginal cost allowed by existing technologies. In this case, a shift in sources of supply from relatively high-cost producers to relatively low-cost producers, driven perhaps by an unleashing of consumer demand, would lower the total economic cost of providing the good, thereby raising the overall economic surplus.

A policy issue raised by the small business expensing allowance concerns its effect on the allocation of resources in general and the allocation of investment capital within the private sector in particular. In theory, all taxes except lump-sum taxes lead to inefficient economic outcomes because they sway the decisions of consumers and producers in ways that leave one group or the other—or both—worse off. Non-lump-sum taxes have this effect because they inevitably distort the economic choices facing individual and business taxpayers, leading them more often than not to allocate resources on the basis of how taxes affect the cost and benefit of the goods and services they buy and sell, rather than according to their actual costs and benefits. Such a distortion entails what economists call a deadweight loss, which is a condition where the amount of revenue raised by a tax is less than the loss of economic welfare it engenders.

The expensing allowance could affect the allocation of resources in an economy by encouraging firms to invest in assets that qualify for the allowance, possibly at the expense of other, more productive assets. There are two channels through which the allowance can produce such an inefficient outcome. One channel is a reduction in the user cost of capital for investment in qualified assets relative to investment in all other assets. A second channel is a temporary increase in the cash flow or retained earnings of firms that acquire qualified assets. Restraining the allowance's influence on the allocation of resources is its phaseout threshold, which effectively confines the benefits of the allowance to relatively small firms.[3]

Not surprisingly, the user cost of capital plays a major role in a firm's investment decisions. This cost embraces both the opportunity cost of an investment and its direct costs, such as depreciation, the actual cost of the asset, and income taxes. In effect, the user cost of capital establishes the after-tax rate of return an investment must earn in order to be profitable—and thus worth undertaking. In general, the higher the user cost of capital, the fewer projects a firm can profitably undertake, and the lower its desired capital stock. When a change in tax policy decreases the user cost of capital, it is reasonable to expect many firms to respond by increasing the amount of capital they wish to own, boosting overall business investment in the short run.

So how does expensing affect the user cost of capital? Expensing is the most accelerated form of depreciation. Under expensing, the entire cost of an asset is written off in its first year of use, regardless of the asset's economic or useful life. Allowing a firm to expense its acquisition of an asset is akin to the U.S. Treasury providing the firm with a tax rebate equal to the firm's marginal tax rate multiplied by the cost of the asset. Accelerated depreciation—along with other investment tax subsidies such as an investment tax credit—reduces the user cost of capital by lowering the pre-tax rate of return on investment a firm must earn in order to realize a particular after-tax rate of return.[4] Expensing yields the largest possible reduction in the user cost of capital from accelerated depreciation. As some studies have shown, this reduction can be considerable.[5]

How beneficial is expensing? One way to illustrate the tax benefit from expensing is to assess how it affects the marginal effective tax rate on the returns to investment in an asset whose cost is expensed. Expensing has the effect of taxing the stream of income earned by an asset over its lifetime at a marginal effective rate of zero.[6] This is because expensing reduces the after-tax return and cost for an investment by the same factor, which is an investor's marginal tax rate. For example, if the income received by a small business owner is taxed at a rate of 35% and the cost of a depreciable asset he or she buys is recovered through expensing, then the federal government effectively becomes a partner in the investment with an interest of 35%. Through the tax code, the federal government assumes 35% of the cost of the asset by allowing its entire cost to be deducted in the first year of the asset's use, and it receives 35% of the income earned by the investment in subsequent years. Conversely, expensing allows the small business owner to receive 65% of the returns from the investment but to bear only 65% of the cost. Such an outcome implies that for each dollar spent on the asset, the owner earns the same rate of return after taxes as before taxes.[7] This equivalence implies that expensing results in an effective marginal tax rate of 0.

Expensing could also spur a rise in business investment by augmenting the cash flow of firms that rely heavily on retained earnings to finance their investments.[8] Expensing can increase a firm's cash flow in the short run because it allows the firm to deduct the full cost of qualified assets in the tax year the firm places them into service. There are several reasons why a firm's investments could depend on its cash flow. One is that the firm's owners or senior managers want to limit their exposure to external debt and the risk of default it entails. Another reason is that the firm has limited or virtually no access to debt and equity markets, because potential investors and lenders lack sufficient information about the firm's products and competitive strategies. For firms in such a position, the cost of internal funds could be lower than the cost of external funds, in which case the firm clearly would be better off financing its investments out of retained earnings.

Nevertheless, the impact of increases in cash flow on business investment remains uncertain. Some studies found a significant positive correlation between changes in a firm's net worth and its investment spending.[9] This correlation was strongest for firms that had very limited access to debt and equity markets. Yet it would be a mistake to interpret these findings as proof that firms with relatively high cash flows invest more than firms with relatively low or negative cash flows. After all, a strong correlation between two factors does not prove the existence of a cause-andeffect relationship between them. It may be the case that firms with relatively high cash flows invest more, on average, than firms with relatively low cash flows for reasons that have little or nothing to do with the relative cost of internal and external funds. The relationship between cash flow and business investment is complicated, and further research is needed to clarify it.

Has the expensing allowance made significant contributions to shifts in the size and composition of the domestic capital stock in the 25 years the allowance has existed in its present form? This question is difficult to answer, largely because there are no studies analyzing the impact of the allowance on capital formation over time, and available empirical evidence is incomplete. Given that the expensing allowance lowers the cost of capital and may boost cash flow for firms using it, and that investment in many of the assets eligible for the allowance seems somewhat sensitive to changes in the cost of capital, one might be justified in concluding that the allowance has caused domestic investment in those assets to be greater than it otherwise would have been.[10] But there are some compelling reasons to argue that much of this investment would have taken place without the expensing allowance.[11] Most economists would be likely to agree that investment in assets eligible for the expensing allowance is driven more by expectations for future growth in sales by firms that purchase these assets, the nature of the assets, and conditions in debt and equity markets than by tax considerations.[12] This view finds some support in available data on use of the expensing allowance: although 22% of corporations filing federal tax returns claimed the allowance from 1999 through 2003, the total value of IRC Section 179 property placed in service in that period was equal to only 5% of domestic gross investment in equipment and computer software. [13]

When seen through the lens of conventional economic theory, the expensing allowance has efficiency effects that may worsen the deadweight loss caused by the federal tax code. Under the reasonable assumption that the amount of capital in the economy is fixed in the short run, a tax subsidy like the allowance is likely to lure some capital away from highly profitable uses and into tax-favored uses. Conventional economic theory holds that in an economy free of significant market failures and dominated by competitive markets, a policy of neutral or uniform taxation of capital income minimizes the efficiency losses associated with income taxation. But the expensing allowance encourages investment in specific assets by relatively small firms. Such a subsidy can interfere with the flow of financial capital to its most profitable uses by making it possible for business owners to earn higher after-tax rates of return on investment in assets eligible for the allowance than on investment in other assets with higher pre-tax rates of return.

In addition, the expensing allowance gives smaller firms an incentive to limit their growth. This unintended effect stems from the rise in marginal effective tax rates on the income earned by an asset eligible for the allowance in the allowance's phaseout range ($530,000 to $663,000 in 2009).[14] Douglas Holtz-Eakin, a former Director of the Congressional Budget Office, has called this incentive effect a "tax on growth by small firms."[15]

## Equity Effects

Equity is another basic concept in conventional economic analysis. It generally refers to the distribution of income among the individuals or households in a particular geographic area.

In the context of income taxation, equity usually denotes the distribution of the tax burden among taxpayers divided into income groups. Economists who analyze the equity effects of income taxes tend to focus on two distinct kinds of equity: horizontal equity and vertical equity. A tax is said to be horizontally equitable if it imposes similar burdens on individuals with similar incomes or living standards. And a tax system is said to be vertically equitable if the burdens it imposes vary according to an individual's or household's ability to pay. The principle of vertical equity lays the foundation for a progressive income tax system. Under such a system, an individual's tax liability, measured as a fraction of income, rises with income.

The current federal income tax system arguably leans more in the direction of vertical equity than horizontal equity. Many individuals with similar incomes before taxes end up being taxed at the same marginal rate. But because so many tax preferences in the form of deductions, preferential rates, deferrals, exclusions, exemptions, and credits have been enacted in recent decades, a significant share of individuals with similar before-tax incomes end up being taxed at different rates. At the same time, those with relatively high pre-tax incomes are generally taxed at higher rates than those with relatively low pre-tax incomes.

How does the expensing allowance affect vertical and horizontal equity?

To answer this question, it is necessary to consider the tax benefits associated with the expensing allowance, who receives them, and how they affect the recipients' federal income tax burdens. The main tax benefit from the allowance is a reduction in the *marginal effective tax rate* on the income earned by assets eligible for expensing. How much of a reduction depends critically on the proportion of an asset's cost that is expensed. As was noted earlier, if the entire cost is expensed, then the marginal effective rate falls to zero. Yet the allowance does not change the *actual marginal rates* at which this income is taxed. This is because accelerated depreciation does not reduce the total amount of taxes (measured in current dollars) owed on the stream of income earned by an asset over its useful life. Rather, accelerated depreciation simply moves forward the timing of depreciation deductions in a way that substantially raises the present discounted value of the tax savings from depreciation deductions.

Most of the assets eligible for the allowance are held by smaller firms. Therefore, it seems reasonable to conclude that most of the tax savings attributable to the allowance ends up in the pockets of small business owners. But such a conclusion is somewhat misleading, as the allowance does not alter the income tax rates that apply to the income earned by small business owners—and thus has no direct effect on the distribution of the federal income tax burden among income groups. Nonetheless, the allowance does lower the tax burden on the returns to a portion of small business investment, which means that the allowance may indirectly violate the principle of vertical equity by decreasing the effective tax rate on income earned by small business owners.

## Tax Administration

Yet another policy question raised by the expensing allowance concerns its impact on the cost of tax compliance for business taxpayers.

Most public finance economists agree that a desirable income tax system is one that imposes relatively low costs for administration and compliance. Research indicates that the administrative cost of a tax system hinges on three factors: (1) the records that must be kept in order to comply with tax laws, (2) the complexity of those laws, and (3) the types of income subject to taxation.

Most public finance economists also agree that the current federal income tax system fails this test. In their view, the costs of collecting income taxes and enforcing compliance with the tax laws are needlessly high, and the primary cause is the growing complexity of the federal tax code. Many small business owners have long complained about the costs imposed on them by the record keeping and filings required by the federal income tax.

The expensing allowance addresses this concern by simplifying tax accounting for the firms that claim it. Less time and paperwork are involved in writing off the entire cost of a depreciable asset in its first year of use than in writing off that cost over a longer period using allowable depreciation schedules. At the same time, the rules governing the use of the regular allowance and the use of the allowance in special areas like EZs and RCs add a layer of complexity to the administration of the tax code by the IRS.

Tax simplification is a longstanding policy objective for a majority of small business owners. A primary motivation for this quest is the relatively high costs small firms evidently bear in complying with federal tax laws. These costs were the main focus of a 2001 study prepared for the Office of Advocacy at the Small Business Administration. The study found that the cost per U.S. employee for tax compliance in 2000 was an estimated $665 for all firms, $1,202 for firms with fewer than 20 employees, $625 for firms with 20 to 499 employees, and $562 for firms with 500 or more employees.[16] This finding appears to lend further support to what is regarded as a well-established truth about the costs to firms of tax compliance: namely, that these costs are[17] regressive to firm size in that "as a fraction of any of a number of size indicators, the costs are lower for larger companies."

## End Notes

[1] The allowance is indexed for inflation in 2004 through 2010. In 2003, it was $100,000; in 2004, $102,000; in 2005, $105,000; in 2006, $108,000; in 2007, $125,000; and in 2008, $250,000. The large increase in 2008 was temporary and resulted from a provision in the Economic Stimulus Act of 2008.

[2] Like the maximum expensing allowance, the phase-out threshold is indexed for inflation in 2004 through 2010. In 2003, the threshold was $400,000; in 2004, $410,000; in 2005, $420,000; in 2006, $430,000; in 2007, $500,000; and in 2008, $800,000.

[3] According to unpublished IRS estimates, a total of $55.161 billion in assets eligible for the IRC Section 179 expensing allowance were placed in service in 2003. Firms with assets of $10 billion or less accounted for 49% of this investment, whereas firms with assets of $100 billion or more accounted for 16%.

[4] The user cost of capital is the real rate of return an investment project must earn to be profitable. In theory, a firm will undertake an investment provided the after-tax rate of return exceeds or at least equals the user cost of capital. Rosen has expressed this cost in terms of a simple equation. Let **C** stand for the user cost of capital, *a* for the purchase price of an asset, *r* for the after-tax rate of return, *d* for the economic rate of depreciation, *t* for the corporate tax rate, *z* for the present value of depreciation deductions flowing from a $1 investment, and *k* for the investment tax credit rate. Then $\mathbf{C} = a \times [(r+d) \times (1-(t \times z)-k)]/(1-t)$. Under expensing, *z* is equal to one. By plugging assumed values for each variable into the equation, one sees that **C** increases as *z* gets smaller. Thus, of all possible methods of depreciation, expensing yields the lowest user cost of capital. For more details, see Harvey S. Rosen, *Public Finance*, 6th ed (New York: McGraw-Hill/Irwin, 2002), pp. 407-409.

[5] In a 1995 study, Douglas Holtz-Eakin compared the cost of capital for an investment under two scenarios for cost recovery. In one, the corporation making the investment used expensing to recover the cost of the investment; and in the other, the cost was recovered under the schedules and methods permitted by the modified accelerated cost recovery system. He further assumed that the interest rate was 9%, the inflation rate 3%, and the rate of economic depreciation for the asset acquired through the investment 13.3%. Not only did expensing substantially reduce the cost of capital, its benefit was proportional to the firm's marginal tax rate. Specifically, Holtz-Eakin found that at a tax rate of 15%, expensing lowered the cost of capital by 11%; at a tax rate of 25%, the reduction was 19%; and at a tax rate of 35%, the cost of capital was 28% lower. See Douglas Holtz-Eakin, "Should Small Businesses Be Tax-Favored?" *National Tax Journal*, September 1995, p. 389.

[6] For a discussion of the economic logic behind such an outcome, see Jane G. Gravelle, "Effects of the 1981 Depreciation Revisions on the Taxation of Income from Business Capital," *National Tax Journal*, March 1982, p. 5.

[7] Raquel Meyer Alexander, "Expensing," in *The Encyclopedia of Taxation and Tax Policy*, Joseph J. Cordes, Robert D. Ebel, and Jane G. Gravelle, eds. (Washington: Urban Institute Press, 2005), p. 129.

[8] In the realm of business finance, the term "cash flow" can take on different meanings. Here it denotes the difference between a firm's revenue and its payments for all the factors or inputs used to generate its output, including capital equipment.

[9] For a review of the recent literature on this topic, see R. Glenn Hubbard, "Capital Market Imperfections and Investment," *Journal of Economic Literature*, vol. 36, March 1998, pp. 193-225.

[10] Two studies from the 1990s found that a 1% decline in the user cost of capital was associated with a rise in business equipment spending of 0.25% to 0.66%. See CRS Report RL3 1134, *Using Business Tax Cuts to Stimulate the Economy*, coordinated by Jane G. Gravelle, p. 4.

[11] There is some anecdotal evidence to support this supposition. At a recent hearing held by the House Small Business Subcommittee on Tax, Finance, and Exports, Leslie Shapiro of the Padgett Business Services Foundation stated that expensing "may be an incentive in making decisions to buy new equipment, but it's not the dominant force." His firm provides tax and accounting services to over 15,000 small business owners. See Heidi Glenn, "Small Business Subcommittee Weighs Bush's Expensing Boost," *Tax Notes*, April 7, 2003, p. 17.

[12] See Roger W. Ferguson, Jr., "Factors Influencing Business Investment," speech delivered on October 26, 2004, available at http://www.federalreserve.gov/boarddocs/speeches/2004/20041026/default.htm.

[13] Various data on business claims for the expensing allowance were obtained via e-mail from the Statistics of Income Division at IRS on March 21, 2006.

[14] Jane Gravelle of CRS has estimated that, with a corporate tax rate of 28% and a rate of inflation of 3%, the marginal effective tax rate on the income earned by assets eligible for the expensing allowance is 36% in the phase-out range for the allowance. By contrast, under the same assumptions, the marginal effective tax rate on the income earned by qualified assets is 0% for each dollar of investment in those assets up to $430,000.

[15] U.S. Congress, Senate Committee on Finance, *Small Business Tax Incentives*, hearings on S. 105, S. 161, S. 628, S. 692, S. 867, and H.R. 1215, 104th Cong., 1st sess., June 7, 1995 (Washington: GPO, 1995), pp. 11-12.

[16] W. Mark Crain and Thomas D. Hopkins, *The Impact of Regulatory Costs on Small Firms* (Washington: Office of Advocacy, Small Business Administration, 2001), p. 32.

[17] Joel Slemrod, "Small Business and the Tax System," in *The Crisis in Tax Administration*, Henry J. Aaron and Joel Slemrod, eds. (Washington: Brookings Institution Press, 2004), p. 81.

In: Small Business Tax Issues and Benefits ISBN: 978-1-61668-806-6
Editors: Alton E. Kastenberg © 2010 Nova Science Publishers, Inc.

*Chapter 3*

# SMALL BUSINESS TAX BENEFITS: OVERVIEW AND ECONOMIC RATIONALE

*Gary Guenther*

## SUMMARY

The federal tax burden on small firms and its effects on their performance and rates of formation and growth is a policy issue that never seems to disappear from Congress's legislative agenda. Continuing congressional interest in the issue has led to the enactment of a series of legislative initiatives to reduce this burden in recent Congresses. In February 2009, the 111th Congress passed a bill (the American Recovery and Reinvestment Act of 2009, P.L. 111-5) intended to spur an economic recovery; it included several small business tax preferences.

This report describes the main federal tax benefits for small firms and examines the economic arguments for and against them. It will be updated as needed.

While a comprehensive estimate of the federal revenue cost of existing small business tax preferences cannot be made with available information, estimates by the Joint Committee on Taxation and the Treasury Department of the revenue lost because of the larger federal tax expenditures indicate that this cost will exceed $15 billion in FY2009. The following small business tax benefits appear to have the widest reach outside the agricultural sector: the taxation of small firms as passthrough entities; the graduated rate structure for the corporate income tax; the expensing allowance for equipment under Section 179 of the Internal Revenue Code; the exemption of some small corporations from the corporate alternative minimum tax; cash-basis accounting; a tax credit for costs incurred by small firms in establishing pension funds for employees; a tax credit for costs incurred by small firms in complying with the Americans with Disabilities Act; and the exclusion from taxation of capital gains on the sale or disposition of qualified small business stock.

These and other small business tax benefits raise some significant policy issues. For economists who specialize in public finance, a key issue is whether or not preferential tax treatment for small firms can be justified on economic grounds. If such a justification cannot be found, then proposals to extend or enhance small business tax preferences arguably could create more economic problems than they solve.

Proponents of granting tax relief to small firms say such relief is justified on several grounds. First, in their view, small firms create opportunities for social and economic advancement. Second, proponents maintain that the rate of small business formation responds favorably to reductions in tax burdens. Third, they note that small firms make important contributions to economic growth and employment over time. Fourth, small firms are thought to face special constraints on their ability to raise needed capital in debt and equity markets. Finally, proponents argue that tax preferences are needed to offset the financial burden placed on small firms as a result of complying with a variety of federal regulations.

Critics of small business tax preferences find it difficult to justify them on economic grounds. They say such preferences lessen the progressivity of the federal income tax and boost the returns on small business investment in ways that distort the domestic allocation of economic resources. In addition, critics contend that many existing small business tax preferences are inappropriate or poorly designed (or in some cases, both), magnifying any efficiency losses associated with them.

Some policy issues never seem to disappear from Congress's legislative agenda. One such issue is the federal tax burden on small firms and its effect on their formation, performance, and growth.

It appears that many lawmakers regard small firms in general as a vital and unsurpassed source of job creation, economic opportunity, and technological innovation. Many of these same individuals are also inclined to see current federal taxation of small firms both as an obstacle to their formation and a drag on their growth, and as an effective policy tool for boosting their rates of formation and growth. Recent Congresses have passed numerous laws that have included a variety of tax preferences for small firms. The 111$^{th}$ Congress has already proven to be no exception. In February 2009 it passed legislation (the American Recovery and Reinvestment Act of 2009, P.L. 111-5) to stimulate the economy that included several tax benefits targeted at small firms. Numerous other bills to extend or enhance existing small business tax benefits, or create new ones, have been introduced.

Existing small business tax benefits and proposals to enhance or expand them raise several policy issues. For most economists, a key policy issue is whether the benefits can be justified on economic grounds. If such a rationale cannot be found, or if the one set forth by proponents of small business tax benefits can be shown to rest on untenable assumptions, then critics of these benefits could be right in arguing that they damage social welfare in the long run. Another policy issue tied to small business tax benefits concerns the use of preferential tax treatment to extend assistance to small firms. The benefits entail costs in the guise of foregone tax revenues and the resources required on the part of the federal government to administer the tax benefits, and on the part of eligible small firms to comply with their requirements. Some question whether tax subsidies are more cost-effective than alternative approaches to providing assistance to small firms, such as grants, loan guarantees, and exemptions from certain federal regulations.

This report explores these issues by examining the main non-agricultural small business tax preferences and the economic arguments for and against them. It begins with a brief description of existing preferences for small firms, then reviews what is known about the economic contributions of small firms, and concludes with a discussion of the principal economic arguments for and against these subsidies.

## FIRM SIZE: HOW SMALL IS SMALL?

When examining the ways in which the federal tax code confers benefits on small firms and what is known about the economic role of small firms, a critical analytical and policy issue is the definition of a small firm.

It turns out that there is no standard or uniform definition of a small firm underlying the host of federal laws and regulations offering assistance to small business. Instead, several criteria are used to identify the firms that qualify for the benefits. Why such variation prevails is difficult to discern from the language of these laws and regulations.

The absence of a standard definition of a small firm may reflect the lack of a consensus among economists and other analysts on what constitutes a small firm. But this absence may also have its roots in the Small Business Act (P.L. 85-53 6, as amended). The act defines a small firm as "one that is independently owned and operated and which is not dominant in its field of operation.[1]" It also notes that the definition of a small firm can vary from industry to industry to reflect important structural differences among industries.[2] Under the act, the Small Business Administration (SBA) has the authority to establish or alter the size standards and limits for determining eligibility for federal programs to assist small business, some of which are administered by the SBA. All federal agencies administering programs that reserve a share of their procurement contracts for small firms are required to use SBA size standards and limits. For other federal programs or statutes offering support for small business, the definition of a qualified firm does not necessarily have to conform to SBA size standards and limits.

In general, three criteria are used to identify the firms eligible for federal small business support programs. Each specifies the maximum size a firm (including affiliates) can attain and still take advantage of the benefits offered by the programs.

For the most part, the SBA uses two criteria to determine eligibility for the programs it administers: (1) number of employees and (2) average annual receipts in the previous three years. Application of these criteria can vary by industry. For example, the sole criterion for most manufacturing and mining firms is employment size, and the upper limit is 500 employees; by contrast, for most retail and service firms, the sole criterion is average annual receipts, and the upper limit is $6 million. SBA's current size limits for small firms range from $0.75 million to $28.5 million for average annual receipts, and from 100 to 1,500 for number of employees.[3]

The SBA Administrator has the authority to modify size standards for particular industries. Before a proposed change can take effect, SBA's Office of Size Standards (OSS) is required to undertake an analysis of the likely impact of the change on the performance of the affected industry or industries—focusing on the degree of competition, average firm size, start-up costs, barriers to entry, and the distribution of sales and employment by firm size—and use the results to make recommendations to SBA's Size Policy Board. If the board agrees with OS S's recommendations, then it normally advises the Administrator to approve the proposed change.

A third criterion used by federal agencies is asset size. Under this standard, eligible firms would hold assets up to a certain threshold, such as $50 million. Among federal programs offering support to small business, use of this criterion is less frequent than number of employees or average annual receipts.

How does the federal tax code define a small firm? Again, there is no uniform or standard definition. Instead, several criteria are used to determine eligibility for current small business tax preferences. Again, it is not clear why the criterion varies from one preference to the next.[4] Some preferences rely on asset size, receipt size, or employment size to select eligible firms. Others confer benefits on small firms not through a mandatory size standard but through the design of the preference itself. A case in point is the small business expensing allowance under Section 179 of the Internal Revenue Code (IRC): although in principle allowance may be claimed by firms of all employment, receipt, or asset sizes, its design effectively confines its benefits to relatively small firms, as is discussed below.

The lack of a standard definition of a small firm in the federal tax code has its advantages and disadvantages. On the one hand, it can lead to a situation where a firm is eligible for some small business tax preferences but not for others, perhaps undercutting the incentive effect of at least some of them. On the other hand, the absence of a standard definition might give lawmakers greater flexibility in crafting tax benefits for small firms that mesh with larger policy objectives.

## MAIN FEDERAL TAX BENEFITS FOR SMALL BUSINESS

In general, all business income is subject to federal taxation, but not all business income is treated the same way under the federal tax code.

The taxation of business income depends on several considerations. One is whether or not a firm is organized for tax purposes as a corporation. Corporate net income eventually is taxed twice (once at the firm level and a second time at the shareholder level), whereas the net income of passthrough entities such as S corporations, sole proprietorships, limited liability companies, or partnerships is taxed only once (at the shareholder level).

In addition, the taxation of business income depends on whether or not a corporation or the owners of passthrough entities pay the alternative minimum tax (AMT). Corporations or business owners paying the AMT may or may not be taxed at lower marginal rates than the rates they would be subject to under the regular corporate income tax.

The tax burden on business income also can vary according to how investments are financed. Corporations may deduct interest payments from taxable income but not dividend payments. As a result, the returns to corporate investments financed solely by debt are taxed at lower marginal effective rates than the returns to investments financed solely by equity.

Firm size is another factor that can affect the tax treatment of business income. Various provisions of the federal tax code offer benefits to smaller firms that are not available, or are of lesser value, to larger firms. The code makes no explicit or formal distinction between the taxation of small and large firms in that it has no separate sections for small and large firms. Rather, there are provisions scattered throughout its many chapters that confer preferential treatment on relatively small firms only. Most of these provisions come in the form of deductions, exclusions and exemptions, credits, deferrals, and preferential tax rates. In general, tax preferences such as these lower the cost of capital for new investment by eligible firms relative to other firms. Some of the provisions benefit small firms by reducing the cost and burden of complying with tax laws, or by making tax relief contingent on providing certain fringe benefits to employees.

The federal tax subsidies targeted exclusively at smaller firms and with the widest reach outside agriculture are described below. Excluded from the list are subsidies available only to small firms in particular industries, such as life insurance, banking, and energy production or distribution. Nor does the list include subsidies from which many small firms derive significant benefits but that are also available to large firms, such as the research and work opportunity tax credits.

It is not known what the total revenue cost is for the subsidies discussed below. Nevertheless, recent estimates by the Joint Committee on Taxation (JCT) and the Treasury Department indicate that they could lower federal revenue in FY2009 by at least $15 billion.[5]

## Taxation of Passthrough Entities

Business enterprises operate in a variety of legal organizational forms. The business laws of each state determine the range of available options. For federal tax purposes, five such forms are widely used: subchapter C corporations, subchapter S corporations, sole proprietorships, partnerships, and limited liability companies (LLCs).

A firm's legal organizational form can have important implications for the taxation of its earnings. The earnings of C corporations are taxed twice: once at the corporate level and again at the individual level when the earnings are distributed to shareholders or owners as dividends or realized capital gains. By contrast, the earnings of all other business entities are taxed only once: at the individual level of their owners or shareholders. As a result, these entities are often referred to as passthrough entities: their earnings escape taxation at the entity level but are passed through to the owners.[6] The entities' profits, losses, items of income, deduction, exclusion, deferral, and credit are attributed to the owners according to their shares of ownership, regardless of whether the profits have been distributed. Most businesses operate as sole proprietorships: in 2005, they accounted for 67% of federal business tax returns. Next in order of magnitude were S corporations (12% of business tax returns), followed by partnerships (9% of returns), C corporations (6% of returns), and farms (6% of returns).[7]

There is no legal requirement that C corporations be relatively large in income, asset or employment size, and that passthrough firms be relatively small. Yet such a difference is the reality: in 2005, for example, the average C corporation's asset size was $32.1 billion, compared to $5 million for the average partnership and $743 million for the average S corporation.[8]

Whether a business owner would be better off operating as a C corporation or as some kind of passthrough entity is a complicated decision involving many tax and non-tax considerations. Key non-tax considerations include the legal liability of shareholders, access to capital markets, and degree of shareholder control of management. Foremost among tax considerations are relative tax rates for corporate income, individual ordinary income, and long-term capital gains; the investment horizon of investors; the holding period for corporate stock; and the rate at which corporate profits are paid out as dividends.

The current mix of individual and corporate tax rates favors passthrough entities by a small margin for investors in the highest income tax bracket. A few simple calculations prove this point. In 2009, the top personal tax rate is 35%; most corporate profits are taxed at 35%; and the top tax rate on long-term capital gains is 15%.[9] Assuming an investment horizon of one year—after which the firm's assets are liquidated—tax considerations alone would dictate that a high-income individual would be better off owning a business enterprise operated as a partnership than as a C corporation. Under such a scenario, after-tax returns to a partnership would be $0.65 for every dollar invested, whereas they would be $0.55 for every dollar invested in a C corporation.[10] Extending the investment horizon to five years does not alter the result. Assuming all after-tax income earned during that period is reinvested in the business, the firm's assets are liquidated after five years, and individuals in the top tax bracket can earn a pre-tax rate of return of 20% whether the business is operated as a partnership or a corporation, a partnership would earn a higher after-tax rate of return than a C corporation: 13.0% versus 11.3%.[11]

Still, it would be incorrect to view the taxation of passthrough entities as a small business tax benefit. This is because a firm's size has no bearing on its ability to operate as a passthrough entity. Some firms that are relatively large in employment, revenue, or asset size are organized as S corporations or partnerships, while some firms that are relatively small in those measures of size operate as C corporations. In 2005, 17% of S corporations and 7% of partnerships filing federal income tax returns reported total receipts of more than $1 million, while 38% of C corporations filing federal income tax returns reported total receipts of $100,000 or less.[12]

Any tax advantage presently held by passthrough entities has proven to be ephemeral in the recent past. For instance, their present advantage would evaporate if legislation were enacted that substantially reduces the top corporate and long-term capital gains tax rates relative to the maximum individual income tax rate. In fact, current tax law could diminish or even extinguish the current appeal of passthrough entities. The individual tax cuts enacted under the Bush Administration are due to expire at the end of 2010. Assuming current law is not changed, beginning in 2011, the maximum individual income tax rate would rise from 35% to 3 9.6%, and the maximum long-term capital gains rate would increase from 15% to 20%.

## Graduated Corporate Income Tax Rates

Corporations with less than $10 million in taxable income are subject to a set of graduated tax rates. The rate is 15% on the first $50,000 of income, 25% on the next $25,000, and 34% on amounts between $75,000 and $100,000 and between $335,000 and $10 million. Corporations with taxable incomes ranging from $10 million to $15 million pay a marginal rate of 35%. In two income ranges, corporations face marginal tax rates greater than 35%: a corporation with taxable income between $100,000 and $335,000 pays a marginal rate of 39%; if its taxable income falls between $15 million and

$18.3 million, the firm pays a marginal rate of 38%. These higher rates are intended to offset the tax savings that firms realized when their tax rates were below 35%. All corporate taxable income above $18.3 million is taxed at a rate of 35%. As a result, the tax savings from the rates of 15% to 34% are limited to corporations with taxable incomes under $335,000.

This rate structure mainly benefits corporations that are relatively small in employment or asset size. It also gives owners of closely held small firms an added incentive to incorporate in order to shield any profits from higher individual tax rates. But not all small corporations are allowed to take advantage of the reduced rates. Specifically, regardless of the amount, the taxable income of corporations providing services in the fields of health care, law, engineering, architecture, accounting, actuarial science, the performing arts, and consulting is taxed at a fixed rate of 35%.

The graduated rate structure has at least one unavoidable drawback: it gives small corporations a disincentive to grow to the point where their net incomes are taxed at marginal rates above 34%. It could be argued that rates above 34% serve as a tax on growth.

The revenue loss arising from the reduced rates on the first $10 million of corporate taxable income could total an estimated $3.3 billion in FY2009.[13]

## Expensing Allowance for Certain Depreciable Business Assets

Expensing is the most accelerated form of depreciation for tax purposes. It entails treating the cost of a depreciable asset such as a machine or building as a current expense rather than as a capital expenditure. Current costs are deducted in the year in which they are incurred, whereas capital costs normally are recovered over longer periods by applying the depreciation methods and schedules allowed in the federal tax code.

Under Section 179 of the Internal Revenue Code (IRC), firms may expense (or deduct) up to $250,000 of the cost of qualified business property—mainly machinery, equipment, and computer software—placed into service in 2008 and 2009, and write off the remaining basis (if any) using a temporary 50% depreciation allowance and current cost recovery rules.[14] The expensing allowance is scheduled to drop to $125,000 in 2010, before adjustment for inflation. Starting in 2011, the maximum allowance will be fixed at $25,000, with no adjustment for inflation.

Owing to a rule known as the dollar limitation, not all firms are able to take advantage of the expensing allowance. Under this limitation, the allowance is reduced by the amount by which the total cost of qualified property placed in service during a year exceeds a phase-out threshold. In 2008 and 2009, this threshold is set at $800,000. It is scheduled to drop to $500,000 in 2010, before an adjustment for inflation. Beginning in 2011, the threshold will be fixed at $200,000, with no adjustment for inflation. So none of a firm's spending on qualified property placed into service in 2009 may be expensed once its total spending on such property exceeds $1,050,000: the $250,000 expensing allowance, plus the $800,000 phase-out threshold.

The allowance has the potential to serve as a robust investment tax subsidy. Because of the phaseout threshold, it mainly benefits firms that are relatively small in revenue, asset, or employment size. Generally, the allowance can stimulate business investment in two ways. First, it can lower the user cost of capital for investment in qualified assets. In theory, expensing produces a zero marginal effective tax rate on the returns to investment in those assets under the standard economic model for the determination of the user cost of capital.[15] Second, the allowance can boost business investment by increasing the cash flow of firms that can take advantage of it. For some firms, the cost of internal funds is lower than the cost of external funds such as loans or equity; so their investment hinges on the availability of internal funds, their cash flow.

The impact of the allowance on the cost of capital is illustrated in a 1995 article by Douglas Holtz-Eakin. Among other things, he assessed the effect of the expensing allowance on a firm's user cost of capital. **Table 1** summarizes his findings.[16] The first column provides the assumed corporate tax rate; the second shows the required pre-tax rate of return if the entire cost of the investment is expensed; the third column gives the required pre-tax rate of return if the entire cost is recovered through the depreciation deductions allowed under federal tax law in the early 1990s; and the final column presents the effective tax subsidy from expensing, which is expressed as the difference (in percentage points) between the required rates of return shown in columns three and two.

At least two conclusions can be drawn from the results. First, expensing offered a significant investment subsidy, and the extent of the subsidy increased with a firm's marginal tax rate. For example, at a tax rate of 15%, expensing lowered the user cost of capital by about 11%; but at a rate of 35%, the reduction jumped to 28%. Second, the user cost of capital under expensing declined as the tax rate increased because tax deductions gain in dollar value at higher tax rates.

In FY2009, the allowance could produce an estimated revenue loss of $6.0 billion.[17] The revenue effects of the expensing allowance in any year depend on the aggregate amount of business investment in qualified assets. In periods of rising investment, the allowance typically leads to a net revenue loss. But when investment falls following a period of expansion, the allowance can actually yield a net revenue gain. This shift from loss to gain is due to the timing of depreciation deductions under current tax law. Firms that can deduct the entire cost of an asset in its first year of use by claiming the Section 179 expensing allowance have no depreciation allowances to deduct from future taxable income generated by the asset.

**Table 1. Estimated User Cost of Capital Under-Expensing (%)**

| Corporate Tax Rate | Expensing | Regular Depreciation | Absolute Size of the Subsidy |
|---|---|---|---|
| 15% | 17.95% | 20.23% | 2.28[a] |
| 25 | 17.05 | 21.13 | 4.08 |
| 35 | 16.15 | 22.40 | 6.25 |

Source: Douglas Holtz-Eakin, "Should Small Business Be Tax-Favored?" *National Tax Journal*, Sept. 1995.

Note: The calculations assume an interest rate of 9%, an inflation rate of 3%, and a rate of economic depreciation of 13.3%. The following formula is used to compute the user cost of capital:

$$c/q = (p - + \delta/1 - \tau)\xi(1 - \tau\xi),$$

where $c$ is the annual value of revenue from the investment, $q$ is the purchase price of the capital good, $p$ is the after-tax financial cost of capital, *pi* is the rate of inflation, $d$ is the rate of geometric depreciation, $t$ is the marginal tax rate, and $z$ is the present value of depreciation allowances per dollar of investment. In the case of expensing, $z = 1.0$; and in the case of regular depreciation, $z = 0.2814$.

a. Percentage points, not percent.

## Exemption of Certain Small Corporations from the Corporate Alternative Minimum Tax

Under current federal tax law, many corporations must compute their income tax liability under both the regular tax and the alternative minimum tax (AMT) and pay whichever is greater. Each tax has its own rates, allowable deductions, and rules for the measurement of taxable income.

In general, the AMT applies a lower marginal rate to a broader tax base. It expands the corporate tax base by adding a number of tax preferences under the regular corporate income tax to taxable income under the AMT. In addition, most tax credits allowed under the regular corporate income tax cannot be used to reduce AMT liability. The current AMT originated with the Tax Reform Act of 1986 and is mainly intended to ensure that all profitable corporations pay at least some federal income tax.

As a result of the Taxpayer Relief Act of 1997 (P.L. 105-34), certain small corporations have been exempt from the AMT since 1998. Eligibility is determined by a corporation's average annual gross receipts in the previous three tax years. All corporations formed after 1998 are exempt from the AMT in their first year with taxable income, regardless of the size of their gross receipts. They remain exempt as long as their average annual gross receipts do not exceed $5 million in their first three tax years, and as long as their average annual gross receipts do not exceed $7.5 million in each succeeding three-year period (e.g., 1999-2001, 2000-2002, etc.). If a corporation loses its eligibility, it becomes subject to the AMT in the first tax year when it no longer qualifies for the exemption and in every tax year thereafter, regardless of the amount of its gross receipts.

There is reason to believe that this exemption gives some eligible small corporations what amounts to a slight competitive advantage over comparable firms paying the AMT. A 1997 study estimated that firms that invested heavily in machinery and equipment and intangible assets like research and development (R&D), financed the bulk of their investments through debt, and paid the AMT for five or more successive years had a higher cost of capital than comparable firms that paid the regular income tax only in the same period.[18]

The exemption also provides owners of small firms with an incentive to incorporate, since the taxable income of passthrough entities is subject to the individual AMT through the tax returns filed by individual owners.

A 2000 report by the Treasury Department's Inspector General for Tax Administration (TIGTA) found that the exemption from the AMT for small firms ran into some unexpected problems during the first year or two it was in effect. According to the report, more than 2,300 small corporations paid the AMT in 1998, even though an examination of their federal income tax returns indicated they qualified for the exemption. Their overpayments of the tax may have totaled more than $25 million.[19] The report attributed the erroneous payments to the many complex changes in the corporate AMT made by the

Taxpayer Relief Act of 1997 and the "short time" available to taxpayers and tax professionals to understand the changes and apply them in filing 1998 tax returns. It recommended the IRS take certain steps to increase taxpayer awareness of the exemption, explain how it was supposed to work, and identify and contact taxpayers who erroneously paid the AMT. In a follow-up study, TIGTA found that the IRS had taken most of these steps, but that the agency had failed to notify the more than 3,600 taxpayers thought to have mistakenly paid the AMT. TIGTA came to the conclusion that the IRS had fallen short of its obligation and promise to "inform and educate tax practitioners on what they need to do on their clients' behalf."[20]

There is no estimate of the revenue cost of exempting small corporations from the AMT, but it is probably less than $10 million a year. While exempt firms do not have to compute their AMT liability, they do pay the regular corporate income tax if their taxable income is positive.

## Amortization of Business Start-Up Costs

A key concept undergirding the federal income tax is that taxable income should exclude all the costs incurred in earning it. This implies that all ordinary and necessary costs paid or incurred in conducting a trade or business should be deducted from a firm's taxable income. The concept also implies that ordinary and necessary costs paid or incurred in connection with starting or organizing a business should not be treated as current expenses, as they were not related to the generation of income. Rather, because these expenses were incurred in an attempt to create an asset (namely, the business) with a useful life extending beyond a single tax year, it stands to reason that they should be capitalized, added to the owner's basis in the business, and recovered when the business is sold or ceases to exist.

But under IRC Section 195 (as amended by P.L. 108-357), business taxpayers who incur business start-up and organizational costs after October 22, 2004, are allowed to deduct up to $5,000 of those costs in the year when the new trade or business begins. This maximum deduction is reduced (but not below zero) by the amount by which eligible expenditures exceed $50,000. Any eligible expenditures that cannot be deducted may be amortized over 15 years, beginning in the month when the new trade or business begins to earn income. In order to claim the $5,000 deduction, a taxpayer must have an equity interest in the new trade or business and actively participate in its management.

Business taxpayers who incurred or paid business start-up and organizational costs and then entered a trade or business on or before October 22, 2004, could amortize (or deduct in equal annual amounts) those expenditures over not less than five years, beginning in the month when the new trade or business commenced.

To qualify for the current deduction, the start-up and organizational costs must meet two requirements. First, they must be paid or incurred as part of an investigation into creating or acquiring an active trade or business, as part of starting a new trade or business, or as part of an activity done to produce income or profit before starting a trade or business with the aim of converting the activity into an active trade or business. Second, the costs must be the similar in kind to costs that would be deductible if they were paid or incurred in connection with the expansion of an active trade or business in the same industry entered by a new firm.

Business taxpayers who choose not to claim the deduction must capitalize all start-up expenses.

The option to deduct as much as $5,000 in business start-up and organizational costs in the first year of operation clearly benefits small start-up firms. It permits the owner of such a firm to deduct expenses in the year when the business begins. Without such a provision, the expenses could not be recovered until the owner sells his or her interest in the business. In effect, the option accelerates the recovery of certain necessary business costs, and this acceleration can aid the growth of small start-up firms by reducing their cost of capital and increasing their cash flow at a time when their access to debt and equity markets may be limited. For firms that lose money in their first year of operation, the deduction can increase their net operating losses for tax purposes, which may be carried back up to two years or forward up to 20 years and used to offset taxes paid or owed.[21]

According to the Joint Tax Committee, the amortization or deduction of qualified business startup and organizational costs could lead to an estimated revenue loss of $0.8 billion in FY2009.[22]

## Cash-Basis Accounting

IRC Section 446 requires firms to compute their taxable income using the same method of accounting they regularly employ in keeping their books, provided that method clearly reflects income. For a business taxpayer's method of accounting to clearly reflect income, it must treat items of income and deductions consistently from one tax year to the next. Permissible methods of accounting include the cash-receipts method, the accrual method, the installment method, the long-term-contract method, the crop method, the special methods for research and development expenditures, and the method for soil and water conservation expenditures.

Two methods of financial accounting are widely used in the private sector: cash-basis and accrual-basis. Under cash-basis accounting, which is the preferred method for self-employed individuals, income generally is recorded when it is received in the form of cash or its equivalent, and expenses generally are recorded when they are paid, regardless of when the income actually is earned or the expenses actually are incurred.

Under accrual-basis accounting, income and expenses generally are recorded when the transactions giving rise to them are completed or nearly completed, regardless of when cash or its equivalent is received or paid. More specifically, a firm using accrual-basis accounting records income when its right to receive it is established, and expenses when the amounts are fixed and its liability for the expenses is established.

Each accounting method has advantages. The principal advantage of cash-basis accounting is that it is much simpler to administer. It also allows firms that use it to control the timing of items of income or deductions. In contrast, accrual-basis accounting often yields a more accurate measure of a firm's economic income because it matches income with expenses with greater precision and rigor.

In general, when an inventory is necessary to the operation of a business, a business taxpayer is required to use the accrual method in computing taxable income — unless the IRS determines that another method clearly reflects income and authorizes its use. Inventories are considered necessary when a firm earns income from the production, purchase, or sale of merchandise. In addition, C corporations, partnerships with C corporations as partners, trusts that earn unrelated business income, and authorized tax shelters generally are required to use the accrual method of accounting.

But there is an exception to this rule. Any partnership or C corporation with average annual gross receipts of $5 million or less in the three previous tax years may use the cash method of accounting. It also may be used by individuals, S corporations, and qualifying partnerships and personal service corporations.

Moreover, even though purchases and sales of inventory items cannot be reported for tax purposes using the cash method of accounting, the IRS has made an exception for sole proprietorships, S corporations, and partnerships that reported average annual gross receipts of $1 million or less in the three previous tax years (IRS Rev. Proc. 2001-10), regardless of the nature of their trade or business. The cash method may also be used by firms with average annual gross receipts of $10 million or less in the three previous tax years, whose main business is providing services or fabricating products according to customer designs or specifications (IRS Rev. Proc. 2002-28).

As these rules indicate, many of the firms permitted to use the cash method are relatively small in receipt size. In effect, this method offers the same benefit to small firms as the expensing allowance under IRC Section 179: the deferral of income tax payments. The federal tax code rests in part on the notion that a firm receives income when it gains the legal right to be paid for something it has provided. But under the cash method of accounting, a firm may delay the recognition of income until cash payments are received, thereby postponing the payment of tax on that income, or lower its tax liability in a year by accelerating payments for expenses such as supplies, repairs, interest, and taxes.

Despite the possible tax benefits to eligible small firms of using the cash method, it may not be in their self-interest to do so when they need to issue accurate and reliable financial reports. Cash-basis accounting can distort a firm's financial position in several ways.[23] First, because it records transactions involving only cash or its equivalent, the method excludes transactions involving exchanges of assets or liabilities. Second, the determination of net income under cash-basis accounting can be manipulated by recording revenues or expenses long before or after goods and services are produced or sold. As a result, small firms seeking to raise capital in debt or equity markets may be better off using accrual-basis accounting.

The Joint Committee on Taxation estimates that the use of cash-basis accounting outside agriculture will result in a revenue loss of $0.9 billion in FY2009.[24]

## Net Operating Losses

A firm incurs a net operating loss (NOL) for tax purposes when its deductions exceed its gross income. As a result, it has no income tax liability in an NOL year. An NOL may be used to obtain a refund of taxes paid in previous years or to reduce or offset future tax liabilities. Under IRC Section 172(b), a business taxpayer is permitted to carry an NOL back to each of the two tax years preceding the NOL year and forward to each of the 20 tax years following that year.

A provision of the American Recovery and Reinvestment Act of 2009 (ARRA, P.L. 111-5) extended the carryback period for NOLs to five years for eligible firms that incurred an NOL in 2008. Only firms with average annual gross receipts of $15 million or less in the NOL year and the two previous tax years may take advantage of the extension. The provision is intended to bolster the cash flow of small firms that have experienced a significant loss of revenue in the current recession.

The Joint Committee on Taxation estimates that the NOL carryback expansion for qualified small firms will produce a revenue loss of $4.7 billion in FY2009.[25]

## Tax Incentives for Private Equity Investment in Small firms

The federal tax code also contains several provisions intended to encourage the investment of equity capital in certain start-up small firms that might otherwise find it difficult to raise the funds needed to finance current operations or expansions. These provisions, which are described below, do so by increasing the potential after-tax returns or reducing the potential after-tax losses on equity investment in such firms. The same tax benefits are not available to individuals who invest in larger established firms.

### *Partial Exclusion of Capital Gains on Certain Small Business Stock*

Two important considerations in determining an individual's income tax liability are the recognition of income as ordinary or capital and the distinction between long-term and short-term capital gains or losses.

A capital gain or loss arises when a capital asset such as a stock or bond is sold or exchanged. If the selling price is greater than the acquisition or purchase price, then the transaction yields a capital gain. Conversely, a capital loss results when the selling price is less than the purchase price.

Capital assets held longer than 12 months and then sold or exchanged give rise to long-term capital gains or losses, whereas sales or exchanges of capital assets held one year or less produce short-term capital gains or losses. Short-term capital gains are considered ordinary income and thus are taxed at regular income tax rates. By contrast, long-term capital gains are considered capital income and thus are taxed in 2009 at rates of 15% for individual taxpayers subject to marginal income tax rates above 15% and 0% for individual taxpayers in the 10% and 15% income tax brackets.

Under IRC Section 1202, non-corporate taxpayers (including partnerships, LLCs, and S corporations) may exclude 50% of any gain from the sale or exchange of qualified small business stock (QSBS) that has been held for over five years. The exclusion rises to 60% if the QSBS has been issued by a qualified corporation based in an empowerment zone. And under a provision of the ARRA, it becomes 75% for QSBS acquired from February 18, 2009, through December 31, 2010, and held for five years

There is a cumulative limit on the gain from stock issued by a single qualified corporation that may be excluded: in a single tax year, the gain is limited to the greater of 10 times the taxpayer's adjusted basis of all QSBS issued by the firm and sold or exchanged during the year, or $10 million—reduced by any gains excluded by the taxpayer in previous years. The remaining gain is taxed at a fixed rate of 28%. As a result, the marginal effective tax rate on capital gains from the sale or exchange of QSBS held longer than five years is 14%: 0.5 x 0.28.

For individuals subject to the AMT, a portion of the excluded gain is treated as an individual AMT preference item, which means that it must be included in the calculation of AMT taxable income. The portion was 42% for QSBS acquired on or before December 31, 2000 and disposed of by May 6, 2003; 28% for QSBS acquired after December 31, 2000 and disposed of by May 6, 2003; and 7% for QSBS acquired after May 6, 2003 and disposed of by December 31, 2008.[26]

To qualify for the partial exclusion, small business stock must satisfy certain requirements. First, it must be issued after August 10, 1993 and must be acquired by the taxpayer at its original issue, either directly or through an underwriter, in exchange for money, property, or as compensation for services rendered to the issuing corporation. Second, the stock must be issued by a domestic C corporation whose gross assets do not exceed $50 million before and immediately after the stock is issued. Third, at least 80% of the corporation's assets must be tied to the active conduct of one or more qualified trades or businesses during "substantially all" of the requisite five-year holding period. Assets used for working capital, start-up activities, or research and development meet the active business test, even if they are devoted mainly to the development of future lines of business. Specialized small business investment companies licensed under the Small Business Investment Act of 1958 also meet the active business test, making their stock eligible for the partial exclusion.

Not all small firms meeting these requirements can take advantage of the partial exclusion. Stock issued by small C corporations primarily engaged in at least one of the following commercial activities do not qualify for the partial gains exclusion: health care, law, engineering, architecture, hospitality, farming, insurance, finance, and mineral extraction. And stock issued by the following small C corporations is not eligible for the partial exclusion: current or former domestic international sales corporations (DISCs), regulated investment companies (RICs), real estate investment trusts (REITs), real estate mortgage investment conduits (REMICs), financial asset securitization investment trusts (FASITs), cooperatives, or C corporations that have claimed the possessions tax credit under IRC Section 936.

The partial exclusion for QSBS is intended to make it easier for small start-up firms in a variety of industries to raise so-called patient equity capital. It does this by increasing the potential after- tax returns an investor can earn on sales or exchanges of QSBS, relative to potential after-tax returns on similar investment opportunities, over five years. Supporters of the partial exclusion say it is needed to overcome the lack of knowledge and deep uncertainty that surrounds the growth prospects of new start-up firms in industries where sizable investments in research and development over an extended period is a key to survival and expansion.

The Jobs and Growth Tax Relief Reconciliation Act of 2003 (JGTRRA) substantially diluted the incentive effect of the partial exclusion. Before the act, the maximum tax rate on long-term capital gains was 20% on assets held for at least one year and 18% for assets acquired after December 31, 2000 and held for more than five years. By contrast, under the partial exclusion, the effective tax rate on capital gains realized on sales or exchanges of QSBS has always been 14%. Though JGTRRA unified and lowered the maximum tax rate on long-term capital gains to 15%, it made no compensatory change in the taxation of capital gains for QSBS. Thus, a potential buyer of QSBS in the highest tax bracket must evaluate whether the slight difference in rates is worth the risks associated with owning the stock of new unproven firms for a minimum of five years.

An estimated $0.5 billion in revenue will not be collected in FY2009 because of the exclusion.[27]

### *Losses on Small Business Investment Company Stock Treated as Ordinary Losses without Limitation*

Generally, losses on investments in stock are treated as capital losses for tax purposes. These losses may be used to offset any capital gains in the same tax year, but individuals may also use any combination of short-term and long-term capital losses to offset up to $3,000 in ordinary income in a single tax year.

Under IRC Section 1242, however, individuals who invest in small business investment companies (SBICs) are permitted to deduct from ordinary income all losses from the sale or exchange or worthlessness of stock in these companies. This treatment is intended to foster equity investment in these companies by lowering the after-tax loss on an investment in an SBIC, relative to after-tax losses on similar investments.

SBICs are private regulated investment corporations that are licensed under the Small Business Investment Act of 1958 to provide equity capital, long-term loans, and managerial guidance to firms with a net worth of less than $18 million and less than $6 million in average net income over the previous two years. They use their own capital and funds borrowed at favorable rates through SBA loan guarantees to make equity and debt investments in qualified firms. For tax purposes, most SBICs are treated as C corporations.

There are no known estimates of the revenue loss associated with this small business tax benefit.

***Rollover of Gains into Specialized Small Business Investment Companies***

In general, gains or losses on the sale or exchange of stocks are recognized for tax purposes in the tax year when they are realized.

But under IRC Section 1044, which was created by the Omnibus Budget Reconciliation Act of 1993, individual and corporate taxpayers who satisfy certain conditions are allowed to roll over, free of tax, any capital gains on the sale of publicly traded securities. The proceeds from the sale must be used to purchase common stock or partnership interests in specialized small business investment companies (SSBICs) licensed under the Small Business Investment Act of 1958 within 60 days of the sale. SSBICs are similar to SBICs except that SSBICs are required to invest in small firms owned by individuals who are considered socially or economically disadvantaged—mainly members of minority groups.

If the proceeds from the sale exceed the cost of the SSBIC stock or partnership interest, the excess is recognized as a capital gain and taxed accordingly. The taxpayer's basis in the SSBIC stock or partnership interest is reduced by the amount of any gain from the sale of securities that are rolled over. The maximum gain an individual can roll over in a single tax year is the lesser of $50,000 or $500,000 less any gains previously rolled over under this provision. For corporations, the maximum deferral in a tax year is the lesser of $250,000 or $1 million less any previously deferred gains.

There are no known estimates of the revenue loss associated with this small business tax benefit.

### *Ordinary Income Treatment of Losses on Sales of Small Business Stock*

IRC Section 1244 allows taxpayers to deduct any loss from the sale, exchange, or worthlessness of qualified small business stock as an ordinary loss, rather than a capital loss. For business taxpayers, ordinary losses are treated as business losses in computing a net operating loss.

To qualify for this treatment, the stock must meet four requirements. First, it must be issued by a domestic corporation after November 6, 1978. Second, the stock must be acquired by an individual investor or a partnership in exchange for money or other property, but not stock or securities. Third, the stock must be issued by a small business corporation, which the statute defines as a corporation whose total amount of money and property received as a contribution to capital and paid-in surplus totals less than $1 million when it issues the stock. Finally, during the five tax years before a loss on the stock is recognized, the firm must have derived more than 50% of its gross receipts from sources other than royalties, rents, dividends, interest, annuities, and stock or security transactions. The maximum amount that may be deducted as an ordinary loss in a tax year is $50,000 (or $100,000 for a couple filing jointly).

This special treatment is likely to lead to an estimated revenue loss of $50 million in FY2009.[28]

## Uniform Capitalization of Inventory Costs

Firms that earn income from the production, purchase, or sale of merchandise are required to maintain inventories in order to determine the cost of goods sold during a tax year. This cost is subtracted from gross receipts in the computation of taxable income. In most cases, the cost of goods sold is determined by adding the value of a firm's inventory at the beginning of the year to purchases of inventory items made during the year and subtracting from that total the value of the firm's inventory at the end of the year.

IRC Section 263A requires business taxpayers engaged in the production of real or tangible property, or in the purchase of real or tangible and intangible property for resale, to "capitalize" (or include in the estimated value of their inventories) both the direct costs of the property included in inventory and the indirect costs that can be allocated to it. This requirement is known as the uniform capitalization rule and was added to the tax code by the Tax Reform Act of 1986. In general, direct costs are considered the material and labor costs tied to the production or acquisition of goods, and indirect costs refer to the other costs incurred through the production or acquisition of goods (e.g., repair and maintenance of equipment and facilities, utilities, insurance, rental of equipment, land, or facilities, and certain administrative costs). Taxpayers have some discretion in assigning indirect costs to production or resale activities, as long as the methods used in the allocation produce reasonable and tenable results for their trade or business.

Nonetheless, some small firms are exempt from the uniform capitalization rule. Specifically, it does not apply to tangible or intangible property acquired for resale by a business taxpayer that had average annual gross receipts of $10 million or less in the three previous tax years.

This exemption is beneficial because eligible firms face lower administrative costs and less complexity in complying with income tax laws and have more control over the timing of business expense deductions, opening up opportunities for the deferral of income tax liabilities.[29]

There are no known estimates of the revenue loss associated with this small business tax benefit.

## Simplified Dollar-Value LIFO Accounting Method for Small Firms

Business taxpayers that maintain inventories to determine the cost of goods sold are required to estimate the value of their inventories at the beginning and end of each tax year. Because doing this item by item is time-consuming and costly, many taxpayers use methods that assume certain item or cost flows.

One such method is known as "last-in-first-out"(or LIFO). LIFO operates on the assumption that the most recently acquired goods are sold before all other goods. Consequently, LIFO assigns the newest unit costs to the cost of goods sold and the oldest unit costs to the ending inventory. The method can be advantageous when the cost of many inventory items is rising, because it yields a lower taxable income and inventory valuation than other methods. There are various ways to apply LIFO. A widely used application is known as the dollar-value method. Under this method, a taxpayer accounts for its inventories on the basis of a pool of dollars rather than specific items. Each pool includes the value of a variety of inventory items and is measured by the dollar value of the inventory items when they were first added to the inventory account; the year when the items are first added is known as the base year. Using the dollar-value method is complicated and costly for most business taxpayers.[30]

But IRC Section 474, which was added to the tax code by the Tax Reform Act of 1986, allows eligible small firms to use a simplified dollar-value LIFO method. It differs from the regular dollar-value method in the way in which inventory items are pooled and the technique for estimating the base-year value of the pools. A firm is eligible to use the simplified method if its average annual gross receipts were $5 million or less in the three previous tax years.

There is no known estimate of the revenue cost of this small business tax benefit.

## Tax Credit for Pension Plan Start-Up Costs of Small Firms

Under IRC Section 45E, qualified small firms may claim a non-refundable tax credit for a portion of the start-up costs they incur in setting up new retirement plans for employees. The credit, which was enacted as part of the Economic Growth and Tax Relief Reconciliation Act of 2001, began in 2002 and originally was scheduled to disappear (or "sunset") after 2010. But a provision of the Pension Protection Act of 2006 permanently extended the credit. It is a component of the general business credit and thus subject to its limitations and rules for carryover.

The credit is equal to 50% of the first $1,000 in eligible costs incurred in each of the first three years a qualified pension is operative. Eligible costs are defined as the ordinary and necessary expenses incurred in administering the plan and informing employees about the plan's benefits and requirements. Qualified plans consist of new defined benefit plans, defined contribution plans, savings incentive match plans for employees, and simplified employee pension plans. Firms with fewer than 100 employees, each of whom received at least $5,000 in compensation in the previous year, are eligible to claim the credit. They can do so only if at least one highly compensated employee participates in the plan.

The credit gives owners of small firms an incentive to establish pension plans for employees by lowering the after-tax cost of setting up and administering these plans in their first three years. Recent surveys have indicated that these costs can serve as a formidable barrier to the creation of pension plans by small employers.

### Tax Credit for Cost of Making a Business More Accessible to the Disabled

Under IRC Section 44, an eligible small firm may claim a non-refundable credit for expenses it incurs to make its business more accessible to disabled individuals. The credit is equal to 50% of the amount of eligible expenditures in a tax year over $250 but not greater than $10,250. In the case of a partnership, this upper limit applies separately at the partnership level and at the partner or individual level; the same distinction holds in the case of a subchapter S corporation. The disabled access credit is a component of the general business credit under IRC Section 38 and thus subject to its limitations.

To qualify for the credit, a firm must satisfy one of two requirements: its gross receipts (less any returns and allowances) in the previous tax year totaled no more than $1 million, or it employed no more than 30 persons on a full-time basis during that year. A worker is considered a full-time employee if he or she works at least 30 hours a week for 20 or more weeks in a calendar year.

Qualified expenses are defined as the amounts an eligible small firm pays or incurs to bring its business into compliance with the Americans With Disabilities Act of 1990 (ADA). They must be reasonable in amount and necessary in light of legal requirements. Eligible expenses include those related to removing architectural, communication, transportation, or physical barriers to making a business accessible to or usable by disabled individuals; providing interpreters or other effective methods of making materials understandable to hearing-impaired individuals; and supplying qualified readers, taped texts, and other effective methods of making materials understandable to visually impaired individuals.

The credit is intended to ease the financial burden on smaller firms of complying with the mandates of the ADA. There is no known estimate of the credit's revenue cost.

## Economic Importance of Small Firms

Available data on small firms indicate they make significant contributions to the performance of the U.S. economy. A critical consideration in measuring and evaluating those contributions is the definition of a small firm. As one might expect, the broader the definition, the larger the economic impact of small firms. This link between the nature of small firms and their economic impact makes it likely that any discussion of the economic importance of these firms rests on an arbitrary assumption about the size of the population of small firms.

When small firms are defined as independent business enterprises with fewer than 500 employees, as the SBA does in publishing data on small business, there are indications that they play a major role in domestic economic output. In 2005, according to the SBA, firms of that size accounted for 99.7% of employers, employed more than 50% of private non-farm workers, and were responsible for 47% of private non-farm compensation (wages, salaries, and benefits). A separate study came to the conclusion that from 1998 to 2004, firms with 500 or fewer employees accounted for about 50% of nominal gross domestic product (GDP).[31] And it appears that small firms generate a large share of the new domestic jobs created each year. According to data reported by the Bureau of Labor Statistics, firms with less than 500 employees accounted for 65% of net new job creation in the non-farm private sector, from the third quarter of 1992 through the first quarter of 2005.[32] In addition, recent research sponsored by the Center for Economic Studies at the U.S. Census Bureau found that new firms accounted for 3% of annual U.S. employment from 1987 to 2005, and that without their contribution, annual net employment growth would have been -1.2%. This finding implied that existing firms (large and small in employment size) were a drag on net job growth in that period and whatever growth happened was due to business formation or the creation of new firms.[33]

Yet a more restrictive definition of a small firm can yield a different picture of the economic importance of small business. According to a recent study by some economists at the Bureau of Labor Statistics, firms with fewer than 100 employees accounted for 45.0% of average quarterly net job growth from June 1990 to September 2005, while firms with fewer than 500 employees accounted for 63.7%.[34]

The economic importance of small firms varies by industry. In 2002, the share of an industry's contribution to GDP attributable to firms with fewer than 500 employees ranged from 20% for information services to 85% for other services.[35]

Most firms start out small in employment size, and the likelihood is remote that a particular small start-up firm will grow into a large, stable, and mostly profitable firm. Two-thirds of start-up firms survive at least two years, and 44% last at least four years.[36] So while hundreds of thousands of new firms typically are formed each year, nearly as many small firms also fail. This constant churning is reflected in the fluctuating contributions of small firms to annual net job creation in the United States.

There are also some indications that small firms have made significant contributions in the past decade or so to the development of new commercial technologies, and that these contributions have varied by industry. According to a 2003 study by CHI Research, Inc., firms with fewer than 500 employees contributed 41% of all patents filed by domestic corporations from 1996 to 2000. The authors also found that firms of that size produced 13 to 14 times as many patents per employee as larger firms in the same period.[37] Small firms in the study filed 25% of the patents related to biotechnology, 19% of the patents related to pharmaceuticals, 11% of the patents related to medical equipment and electronics, and 9% of the patents related to chemicals other than pharmaceuticals.[38]

## ECONOMIC ARGUMENTS FOR AND AGAINST SMALL BUSINESS TAX PREFERENCES

What is known about the economic importance of small firms raises the question of why the subsidies are needed if small firms normally account for substantial shares of domestic employment and output and play significant roles in the commercial development of certain new technologies.

The answer to this question is not unimportant, as small firms received perhaps more than $11 billion in tax benefits in FY2008—in addition to the financial support they received through other federal programs targeted at small business. If the economic arguments made in favor of these tax subsidies turn out to be weak or untenable on theoretical or empirical grounds, then using these resources for other purposes (e.g., reducing the federal budget deficit or raising federal spending on infrastructure improvement or basic research) may lead to higher levels of economic output per capita in the future.

In evaluating the economic arguments made in favor of small business tax benefits, it should be recognized that persuasive non-economic arguments are also raised in support of these benefits. Some lawmakers attach considerable weight to those arguments. A case in point is the notion that small business is an effective vehicle for expanding the middle class because it can lift people out of poverty.

Nevertheless, only the economic arguments for and against small business tax benefits are discussed below.

## Chief Economic Arguments in Favor of the Preferences

Proponents of small business tax subsidies generally cite four economic justifications for them: (1) the special economic role played by small firms; (2) the barriers to their formation and growth in financial markets; (3) the impact of high marginal tax rates on the formation of small entrepreneurial firms, and (4) the unique opportunities for individual economic advancement offered by small business ownership.

### *Special Economic Role of Small Firms*

The economic contributions of small firms are sometimes cited as a reason to extend government support to small business. For example, in remarks made on the Senate floor in 2001 advocating additional tax benefits for small firms, Senator Christopher Bond stated that "small businesses represent more than 99% of all employers, employ 53% of the private work force, create about 75% of the new jobs in this country, ... contribute 47% of all sales in this country, and ... are responsible for 51% of private gross domestic product."[39] By the same token, in 2003, Senator Olympia Snowe urged her colleagues in the Senate to back the creation of more tax benefits for small firms by pointing out that "they (small businesses) represent 99% of all employers, employ 51% of private-sector workforce, provide about 75% of the net new jobs, contribute 51% of the private-sector output, and represent 96% of all exporters of goods."[40]

Some proponents of small business tax subsidies take this view a step further by arguing that small firms are deserving of government support because they generate special economic benefits that larger firms generally cannot replicate. These benefits can be seen in the multitude of jobs and new technologies they create over time, in their innumerable and ever-changing linkages to larger firms in the economic supply chain, and in their contributions to economic renewal and change. The net effect of the special economic benefits generated by small firms is to make the economy grow faster and become more productive.

According to proponents, the efficiency and productivity gains can be seen in evidence that small firms supply certain goods and services more efficiently than large firms. Economist Bo Carlsson has noted that this advantage is apparent in industries where large production runs and falling unit costs are dominant structural features; examples include computers, automobiles, and steel.[41] In industries such as these, small and large firms often specialize in specific products or services. As a result, they tend to interact more as partners or suppliers than as competitors. In Carlsson's view, the dramatic rise in outsourcing among large U.S. firms in the 1990s had the effect of reinforcing and deepening this division in labor between large and small firms. Among the supposed advantages of small firms in the vast and complex supply chain undergirding the U.S. economy are greater flexibility and quickness in responding to new market opportunities and competitive threats.

The belief that small firms can serve as agents of dynamic economic change and technological advance may have its roots in the roles played by small start-up firms in the origins and growth of certain technologically advanced industries like computers and microelectronics. Two notable findings in the recent literature on firm size and technological innovation are that the contribution of small firms to innovation varies by industry, and that their contributions are likely to be most significant in relatively young industries where no firm has accumulated substantial market power.[42] The same literature provides fresh evidence that in certain industries, small start-up firms have proven more adept than large established firms at identifying promising commercial applications for new technologies and exploiting them. During the 1980s and 1990s, many instances of small start-up firms gaining a temporary advantage this way emerged in biotechnology, microelectronics, computer software, and electronic commerce.[43]

Findings such as these have led some economists to conclude that small entrepreneurial firms play a vital and indispensable role in the overall process of economic growth and renewal. They note that economic growth over time is marked by the continuous creation and destruction of jobs and firms. In their view, without the continuous entry of small entrepreneurial firms, this process would slow down to the point that the standard of living would stagnate and perhaps even decline. Carlsson has argued that in the absence of the "heterogeneity and volatility" provided by small start-up firms, "the economy eventually stagnates or even collapses."[44]

### *Opportunities for the Economic Advancement of Immigrants, Women, and Members of Minority Groups*

Proponents of small business tax subsidies also cite the economic benefits of small business ownership for women, minority groups, immigrants, and the communities where they live as an important justification for the subsidies. They argue that owning and managing a small business gives them the opportunities to increase their income and independence and to move into the economic mainstream of the United States.

In addition, proponents claim that women-, minority-, and immigrant-owned small firms benefit their immediate communities and society at large in ways that go beyond direct economic effects. For example, there is evidence that female small business owners are more likely than their male counterparts to encourage openness in workplace communication and decision-making, hire a diverse workforce, put into place desirable child-care programs, and pay full benefits to employees. In addition, families with self-employed women who work out of their homes seem more stable than the average family.[45] And in the case of minority and immigrant groups, small business ownership helps to build tight-knit social networks, providing job and skills training, and creating informal capital markets.[46]

### *Imperfections in Capital Markets*

Yet another economic argument made in favor of small business tax subsidies is that they can ease or offset the barriers facing many small business owners and aspiring entrepreneurs in trying to raise the funds needed to start or expand a business.

If capital markets were truly efficient, then every business investment opportunity offering a pretax rate of return that exceeds the cost of capital would be funded, regardless of the profitability, cash flow, size, or age of a firm. But proponents of government support for small business say that such is not the case for small firms. In their view, many aspiring entrepreneurs are unable to borrow or attract equity capital, largely because lenders and investors lack the information needed to evaluate the profit potential of the proposed venture. As a consequence, small business owners confronted by such a constraint are often forced to finance projects out of their own resources or the resources of friends and family members, or to abandon the dream of owning their own business altogether. In addition, established small business owners facing severe liquidity constraints may have an elevated risk of failure.

For these reasons, proponents maintain that government support is required to enable cash- strapped small firms to gain access to the funds they need to grow.

### *Impact of Progressive Income Taxes*

Supporters of tax relief for small firms also maintain that taxes have a significant effect on three key decisions made by any small business owner: how fast to grow the firm; whether to expand capital investment—and if so, by how much; and whether to hire more employees—and if so, how many? They cite a variety of studies suggesting that as individual or corporate tax rates rise, small firms tend to grow at a slower rate, invest less in new assets, and become less likely to expand employment.[47] In their view, these effects of higher tax burdens are sufficient reason to offer tax breaks to small firms.

***Cost of Tax Compliance***

Some proponents of small business tax preferences argue that they are also justified because of the inordinate costs the federal government imposes on small firms through the numerous regulations (including taxes) they must comply with. In their view, the preferences offset at least some of those costs, which can be highly regressive. In the case of tax laws and regulations, the regressivity lies in the fixed cost of compliance and the measures of size (e.g., sales, assets, or employees) over which that cost is distributed. Proponents maintain that the cost of tax compliance puts small firms at a competitive disadvantage because their cost per employee is much higher than it is for larger firms in the same industries.

## Chief Economic Arguments against the Subsidies

Not everyone agrees with the arguments made by proponents of small business tax preferences to justify them on economic grounds.

Critics of the preferences cite conventional economic analysis as a justification for eliminating most, if not all, of them. Conventional economic analysis holds that government intervention in the economy generally is warranted to correct some market failure. In general, market failures can be thought of as a set of circumstances that prevents or hinders the emergence of an economically efficient outcome. Foremost among the market failures that call for government intervention are a lack of perfect competition, the presence of public goods, positive or negative external effects (or externalities), the existence of incomplete markets, and imperfect information on the part of consumers.[48] Critics of small business tax subsidies say there is no evidence that any such market failure stands in the way of the formation or growth of small firms. In particular, they maintain that there is no evidence that imperfections in capital markets are leading to the formation of too few or to the failure of too many small firms, or that small firms generate external benefits that larger firms cannot replicate. According to critics, in the absence of a market failure, the use of such subsidies is likely to produce undesirable equity and efficiency effects.

### *Equity Concerns*

Proponents of small business tax preferences generally do not refer to their equity effects in defending them on economic grounds.

But to critics, those equity effects provide a reason to oppose the preferences. In their view, small business tax preferences undercut the progressivity of the federal individual income tax. Under a progressive income tax, an individual's tax liability depends on his or her taxable income; so taxpayers with higher taxable incomes pay higher taxes than taxpayers with lower taxable incomes. But small business tax preferences weaken the link between tax burden and income by reducing the tax burden on the earnings of small firms.

Among public finance economists, it is widely thought that individuals, and not firms, ultimately bear the burden of business income taxes, or reap the benefits of tax subsidies. Critics argue that small business tax benefits ultimately increase the after-tax earnings of small firms, which eventually become part of the income of small business owners, whose income and wealth tend to be well above average for U.S. households.[49]

### *Efficiency Concerns*

Critics also assail small business tax subsidies on efficiency grounds. In theory, income taxes reduce social welfare by driving a wedge between the costs and benefits of the many options for consumption and production facing individual consumers and firms. As a result, conventional economic theory holds that the most desirable tax system is one that raises needed revenue without diverting economic resources from their most productive uses. A case in point is a lump-sum tax: it would impose the same tax on all individuals, regardless of income or wealth.

This doctrine of neutrality has important implications for tax policy. First, it implies that the returns to all investments should be taxed at the same rate. Second, the doctrine implies that any tax that is not uniform across firms is likely to damage social welfare.[50] Finally, it implies that taxes should not distort a firm's choice of inputs or its investment or production decisions.

Small business tax preferences, say critics, violate each of these policy prescriptions. In their view, an efficient or desirable allocation of resources can be achieved only if the tax code does not favor small firms over large firms, or unincorporated firms over incorporated firms, or interfere with the natural growth and evolution of firms, or encourage firms to attain a certain asset, employment, or revenue size and grow no further.[51]

A departure from the doctrine of neutral taxation to assist small firms through tax subsidies might be warranted if there were something uniquely valuable about the economic role of such firms, and if that role can achieve its full expression only through targeted government support. Proponents of small business tax preferences claim that small firms consistently create more jobs and spawn more important technological innovations than large firms, and that government support is needed to ensure that they continue to play these roles. But critics question both the premises and policy implications of this claim.

### Small Firms and Job Creation

Critics and proponents alike agree that small firms generally are a robust source of job creation. According to data from the Small Business Administration, small firms created between 60% and 80% all net new U.S. jobs from 1995 to 2005, depending on how the employment size of a small firm is specified.[52]

Critics maintain, however, that for a variety of reasons these data do not necessarily prove that small firms possess a greater job-creating prowess than large firms. To begin with, they note that the data fail to address some important questions about the measurement of job creation and firm size: What does it mean to be small? When should a firm's size be measured? Is gross or net job creation a better indicator of job-creating prowess? And how long should a job last before it is counted as a net new job?

In addition, critics say there is an abundance of evidence that small firms are not consistently better at creating jobs than large firms. First, there appears to be considerable variation over time in the share of new jobs created by small firms. In a widely cited study, David Birch and James Medoff estimated that the share of total net new jobs generated by firms employing 100 or fewer workers varied from about 40% to 140%, depending on the stage of the business cycle.[53] Second, most of the jobs created by small firms result from the formation of new firms, which typically start out small in employment or asset size. Yet many of these jobs do not last a long time, as most new firms fail within their first few years.[54] Third, a few firms accounted for most small business job creation between the late 1980s and early 1990s—Birch and Medoff labeled these firms "gazelles"—and these firms grew swiftly from small to large, and in some cases from large back to small, suggesting that their job-creating ability was unstable at best.[55] Finally, during the 1970s and 1980s, though large firms and plants dominated job creation and destruction in the manufacturing sector, there was no strong, systematic relationship between firm size and net job growth rates.[56]

Critics also contend that even if small firms were to create more jobs than large firms over time, there is no reason to think that government support for small business would generate ever-faster employment growth. Economic analysis shows that the economy generates jobs through what can best be described as a natural process of growth, decline, and structural change; the size distribution of firms seems to be incidental, nothing more than a byproduct of this process. Therefore, the level of national employment over time is the product of a mix of factors that would overwhelm the employment effects of any government support for small business. The key factors are fiscal and monetary policy, consumer spending, business investment, and the difference between U.S. exports and imports.

## Small Firms and Technological Innovation

Research and development (R&D) is the lifeblood of technological innovation, which, in turn, serves as a powerful engine of long-term economic growth and structural change. Economists generally agree that without government support, business investment in R&D would fall short of the socially optimal amount. Left to their own devices, firms are inclined to invest too little in R&D mainly for two reasons. One is that they cannot capture all the returns to R&D investment, as other firms capitalize on the results of research in spite of intellectual property protection. A second reason is that some firms (mainly small start-up firms) lack access to the financial capital needed to undertake planned R&D projects because potential lenders and investors lack the information they need to assess the profit potential of those projects.[57] This predisposition to invest less in R&D than its likely economic benefits would warrant represents a market failure. To remedy this failure, most economists advocate the use of a variety of government policies aimed at spurring increased business R&D investment.

But critics of small business tax subsidies question the notion that government R&D support should be targeted at small firms. They point to evidence demonstrating that both small and large firms develop the new technologies that drive economic growth and structural change. Critics also claim that the same evidence indicates that it is often impossible to disentangle the contributions of one group of firms from the other. According to data from the National Science Foundation (NSF), larger firms perform the vast share of business R&D: in 2005 and 2006, for example, companies with fewer than 500 employees performed 18% of the industrial R&D conducted in the United States, whereas companies with 10,000 or more employees were responsible for 52% of that R&D.[58]

Nonetheless, small firms and large firms each appear to have distinct advantages as agents of technological innovation.[59] On the one hand, small firms may be more likely than large firms to create or dominate a new industry through R&D, and they may be more flexible than large firms in the pursuit of research goals. On the other hand, large firms can more easily raise the funds needed to finance the substantial sunken costs involved in R&D investments and are likely to capture a larger share of the returns to R&D investments through marketing campaigns, the aggressive use of intellectual property protection, and the creation of regional, national, and international distribution, service, and repair networks.

In addition, some studies have looked at the effects of firm size and market structure on innovation.[60] On the whole, they have found that no firm size appears to be ideal for generating new successful commercial technologies. Rather, there is evidence that in some industries, small firms were more innovative than large firms, but in other industries, large firms had a decisive edge in the generation of new technologies.

### *Other Concerns*

Critics also assail small business tax preferences on the grounds that existing ones often poorly serve their intended purposes or are simply ineffective.

One argument made in favor of the subsidies is that the creation of new small firms is needed to prevent the development of monopoly power by large firms. But critics contend that the best way to achieve that result does not involve government support for the formation and growth of small firms. They point out that only a tiny fraction of small start-up firms survive and grow to the point where they pose a serious competitive threat to large, entrenched firms in the same industry. In the view of critics, antitrust law is a much more effective policy tool than small business tax preferences for thwarting the acquisition of monopoly power and other anti-competitive business practices.

Critics also note that if the aim of public policy is to stimulate employment growth, then it seems irrational to offer small firms tax subsidies that lower the cost of capital, and not the cost of labor. The current expensing allowance is a case in point. Such a subsidy lowers the cost of capital relative to the cost of labor, thereby implicitly encouraging small firms to substitute machinery and equipment for labor where technically feasible. In theory, a tax subsidy like the allowance could lead to lower employment than would be the case if the tax code offered no subsidies for the purchase of capital assets.

Yet another concern about small business tax preferences is that they impose an implicit or a hidden tax on business growth. This tax, which is known among public finance economists as the "notch problem," is the inevitable result of the design of many current tax preferences targeted at small firms. Under the typical small business tax preference, firms lose the tax benefit when their workforce, assets, or receipts surpass a designated limit. Such a design obviously creates a disincentive to grow beyond that limit.

The expensing allowance under IRC Section 179 illustrates this problem. In 2003, the maximum allowance was $100,000 and the phaseout threshold $400,000. When a firm increased its investment in assets that qualified for the allowance beyond $400,000, the amount that could be expensed was reduced dollar for dollar—ultimately to zero when total investment reached $500,000. In effect, this design gave firms a significant incentive to invest no more than $100,000 in qualified assets in a single tax year. For any investment, the cost of capital depends in part on the investor's marginal tax rate. Jane Gravelle of CRS estimated that under the expensing allowance for 2003, the marginal effective tax rate on investment in equipment was 0% on the first $100,000, 26% on amounts above $100,000 to $400,000, 43% on amounts above $400,000 to $500,000, and 26% on amounts above $500,000.[61] For a small firm hoping to accelerate its growth, the design of the allowance can increase its cost of capital at a time when its growth is boosting its capital needs.[62]

## CONCLUDING REMARKS

Available economic data suggest that small firms make important contributions to the performance and growth of the U.S. economy. But the magnitude of the contributions depends critically on how a small firm is defined. Under the definition used by the SBA in administering its programs to support small firms, it appears that small business accounts for a majority of private-sector jobs and about half of private-sector output, generates many technological innovations, and serves as an agent of revitalization and structural change in a variety of industries. A more restrictive definition would yield a different picture of the economic importance of small firms.

These contributions arguably seem to undergird the strong support inside Congress for government policies to assist small business. A concrete manifestation of this support is the preferential tax treatment received by many small firms. The combined revenue cost of current federal small business tax subsidies may have exceeded $11 billion in FY2008. Owing largely to the political clout of the small business community and widespread agreement among lawmakers that the federal government should take steps to stimulate the economy, the 111th Congress is likely to consider a variety of initiatives to extend or expand these subsidies.

Still, conventional economic analysis can challenge the view that small business tax preferences are justified on economic grounds. The preferences have the effect of lowering the tax burden on owners of small firms, diluting (to an extent that is difficult to measure) the progressivity of the federal individual income tax system. Furthermore, the preferences seemingly do little to promote growth in productivity and the output of goods and services. In theory, any tax other than a lump-sum tax causes efficiency losses by distorting the behavior of consumers and firms. In the case of production, the best possible outcome is an income tax system that does not distort the production arrangements within firms and taxes all returns to capital at the same rate. Most economists hold that departures from this doctrine of uniform or neutral taxation are warranted only to correct clear and harmful market failures. But in the case of small firms, there is no evidence that a market failure is affecting their formation, performance, or growth in ways that harm social welfare.

This is not to suggest that government support for small firms cannot ever be justified on purely economic grounds. If convincing evidence were to emerge that the formation and growth of small entrepreneurial firms are critical to an efficient allocation of economic resources, and that some market failure was unduly restraining their formation or growth, then even critics might accept that government action to correct the failure would be warranted.

One possible market failure would be imperfections in capital markets that unreasonably denied promising small start-up firms access to the financial capital they need to develop new products and services and grow their business. In theory, this problem could be resolved through a series of policy measures aimed at breaking down the barriers that were preventing these firms from gaining the funding they desired without diverting the overall flow of capital away from its most productive uses. Tax subsidies might be helpful, but to be cost-effective, they would need to address the root causes of the capital market imperfections at a lower economic cost than alternative policy responses, such as increased federal regulation of financial markets or the establishment of a federally subsidized lending facility.

Another possible market failure would involve conclusive evidence that small firms as a whole are more innovative than other firms and thus are responsible for a disproportionately large proportion of the positive externalities arising from technological innovation. It seems improbable that such a market failure would materialize, however, given that these externalities are tied to specific innovations, not to the operations of a specific class of firms.

If anything, the findings of this report suggest the need for a robust model of the process by which small firms are formed and grow and contribute to the total output of goods and services and productivity over time. As the report has suggested, considerable uncertainty still surrounds this process. As some economists have noted, the development of such a model might make it easier for policymakers to determine whether a market failure lies behind any problems facing a wide swath of small firms; identify the key factors contributing to any market failure that is detected; and devise appropriate and cost-effective remedies for the problem. [63] Further research on the economic contributions of small business is needed to develop such a model.

## End Notes

1 15 U.S.C. § 632(a)(1)

2 See U.S. Small Business Administration, *FAQs: Frequently Asked Questions: Size Standards*, available at http://web

3 Ibid.

4 According to one source, the Internal Revenue Code contains at least 24 different definitions of a small business. See Douglas K Barney, Chris Bjornson, and Steve Wells, "Just How Small Is Your Business?," *National Public Accountant*, Aug. 2003, pp. 4-6.

5 In FY2008, the estimated combined revenue loss for six of the small business tax preferences discussed here is $11 billion. It covers the following small business tax preferences: (1) expensing of depreciable business property; (2) reduced rates on the first $10 million of corporate taxable income; (3) cash accounting outside agriculture; (4) the partial exclusion of capital gains on the sale of certain small business stock; (5) the amortization of business start-up costs; and (6) the ordinary income treatment of losses on the sale of small business corporation stock. See U.S. Congress, Joint Committee on Taxation, *Estimates of Federal Tax Expenditures for Fiscal Years 2008-2012*, JCS-2-08 (Washington: GPO, 2008), tables 2 and 3; and Office of Management and Budget, *Analytical Perspectives, Budget of the United States Government, Fiscal Year 2009* (Washington: U.S. Govt. Print. Off., 2008), table 19-1.

6 For more details on the taxation of non-corporate businesses, see CRS Report RL3 1538, *Passthrough Entities Not Taxed As Corporations*, by Jack H. Taylor, available upon request from the author.

7 U. S. Congress, Joint Committee on Taxation, *Tax Reform: Selected Financial Tax Issues Relating to Small Business and Choice of Entity*, JCX-48-08 (Washington: June 4, 2008), table 1, p. 8.

8 Ibid., tables 3 to 5, pp. 14-16.

9 Under the Jobs and Growth Tax Relief Reconciliation Act of 2003 (JGTRRA, P.L. 108-27), in 2003, the top individual income tax rate is 35% and is scheduled to remain at that level

through 2010, and the maximum rate on longterm capital gains is 15% for assets sold after May 6, 2003 and before January 1, 2009.

[10] These tax rates are derived from the following formula: (1-*tp*) is less than or equal to (1- *tc*) x (1- *tcg*), where *tp* is the highest personal tax rate, *tc* is the highest corporate tax rate, and *tcg* is the maximum tax rate on long-term capital gains. See Myron S. Scholes, et. al., *Taxes and Business Strategy: A Planning Approach*, 2nd edition (Upper Saddle River, NJ: Prentice-Hall, Inc., 2001), p. 67.

[11] The after-tax rate of return for a partnership is derived from the following formula: $1 [1 + *R* x (1- *tp*)]$^n$, where *R* is the expected pre-tax rate of return, *tp* is the highest personal tax rate, and *n* is the investment horizon. And the after-tax rate of return for a corporation is derived from the following formula: $1 [1 + *R* x (1- *tc*)]$^n$ (1- *tcg*) + *(tcg* x $1), where *R* and *n* are the same as the previous formula, *tc* is the highest corporate tax rate, and *tcg* is the maximum tax rate on long-term capital gains. See Scholes, *Taxes and Business Strategy*. pp. 66-67.

[12] Joint Committee on Taxation, *Tax Reform: Selected Federal Tax Issues Relating to Small Business and Choice of Entity*, tables 3 to 5, pp. 14-16.

[13] U.S. Congress, Joint Committee on Taxation, *Estimates of Federal Tax Expenditures for Fiscal Years 2008-2012*, JCS-2-08 (Washington: GPO, 2008), p. 71.

[14] The Economic Stimulus Act of 2008 (P.L. 110-185) raised the maximum allowance to $250,000 and the phase-out threshold to $800,000 for 2008 only. The American Recovery and Reinvestment Act of 2009 (P.L. 111-5) extended both limits through the end of 2009. Those limits are higher for firms located in certain economically distressed areas. For more details on the design of the expensing allowance and its economic effects, see CRS Report RL3 1852, *Small Business Expensing Allowance: Current Status, Legislative Proposals, and Economic Effects*, by Gary Guenther.

[15] See Jane G. Gravelle, "Effects of the 1981 Depreciation Revisions on the Taxation of Income From Business Capital," *National Tax Journal*, vol. 35, no. 1, March 1982, pp. 2-6. In effect, under expensing, the after-tax rate of return on an investment becomes equal to the pre-tax rate of return. This happens because expensing reduces costs and after-tax returns by the same proportion, which is determined by the tax rate.

[16] Douglas Holtz-Eakin, "Should Small Businesses Be Tax-Favored?," *Tax Notes*, vol. 48, No. 3, Sept. 1995, p. 389. (In 2003, Dr. Holtz-Eakin was named the Director of the Congressional Budget Office.)

[17] Joint Committee on Taxation, *Estimates of Federal Tax Expenditures for Fiscal Years 2008-2012*, p. 71.

[18] Andrew B. Lyon, *Cracking the Code: Making Sense of the Corporate Alternative Minimum Tax* (Washington: Brookings Institution Press, 1997), pp. 77-97.

[19] U.S. Department of the Treasury, Inspector General for Tax Administration, *More Small Corporate Taxpayers Can Benefit from the Alternative Minimum Tax Exemption Provision*, no. 2001-30-019 (Washington: Nov. 2000), p. 4.

[20] U.S. Department of the Treasury, Inspector General for Tax Administration, *Significant Actions were Taken to Address Small Corporations Erroneously Paying the Alternative Minimum Tax, but Additional Actions Are Still Needed*, no. 2003-30-114 (Washington: May 2003), pp. 4-5.

[21] Under the American Recovery and Reinvestment Act of 2009 (P.L. 111-5), eligible firms with net operating losses in the 2008 tax year may carry them back up to five years. Only firms with average annual gross receipts in the past three tax years of less than $15 million may take advantage of this expanded carryback.

[22] Joint Tax Committee, *Estimates of Federal Tax Expenditures for Fiscal Years 2008-2012*, p. 71.

[23] See Robert Libby, Patricia A. Libby, and Daniel G. Short, *Financial Accounting* (Chicago: Irwin, 1996), p. 111.

[24] Joint Tax Committee, *Estimates of Federal Tax Expenditures for Fiscal Years 2008-2012*, p. 71.

[25] Joint Tax Committee, *Estimated Budget Effects of the Revenue Provisions Contained in the Conference Agreement for H.R. 1, the "American Recovery and Reinvestment Act of 2009,"* JCX-19-09 (Washington: Feb. 12, 2009).
[26] The 7% rate stems from a provision in JGTRRA.
[27] Joint Committee on Taxation, *Estimates of Federal Tax Expenditures for Fiscal Years 2008-2012*, p. 71.
[28] Office of Management and Budget, *Analytical Perspectives: Budget of the U.S. Government in Fiscal Year 2009* (Washington: GPO, 2008), table 19-2, p. 294.
[29] See Paul G. Schloemer, "Simplifying the Uniform Inventory Capitalization Rules," *Tax Notes*, vol. 53, no. 9, Dec. 2, 1991, pp. 1065-1069.
[30] For more details on this method, see U.S. Congress, Joint Committee on Taxation, *Impact on Small Business of Replacing the Federal Income Tax*, JCS-3-96 (Washington, Apr. 23, 1996), pp. 18-19.
[31] Small Business Administration, Office of Advocacy, *Frequently Asked Questions* (Washington: August 2007), and Katherine Kobe, *The Small Business Share of GDP, 1998-2004*, report for the Small Business Administration (Washington: Apr. 2007), pp. 7 and 13.
[32] Department of Labor, Bureau of Labor Statistics, *New Quarterly Data from BLS on Business Employment Dynamics by Size of Firm* (Washington: Dec. 2005), p. 3.
[33] John Haltiwanger, Ron Jarmin, and Javier Miranda, *Business Formation and Dynamics by Business Age: Results from the New Business Dynamics Statistics*, discussion paper, May 2008, p. 14.
[34] Jessica Helfand, Akbar Sadeghi, and David Talan, "Employment Dynamics: Small and Large Firms Over the Business Cycle," *Monthly Labor Review*, Mar. 2007, p. 41.
[35] Katherine Kobe, *The Small Business Share of GDP, 1998-2004*, p. 7.
[36] Small Business Administration, *Frequently Asked Questions*, updated Sept. 2008.
[37] CHI Research, Inc., *Small Serial Innovators: The Small Firm Contribution to Technical Change*, report for the Small Business Administration (Washington: 2003), p 3.
[38] Ibid., p. 17.
[39] Sen. Christopher Bond, remarks in the Senate, *Congressional Record*, daily edition, vol. 147, Jan. 25, 2001, p. S576.
[40] Sen. Olympia Snowe, remarks in the Senate, *Congressional Record*, daily edition, vol. 149, no. 6, Jan. 14, 2003, p. S 299.
[41] Bo Carlsson, "Small Business, Entrepreneurship, and Industrial Dynamics," in *Are Small Firms Important? Their Role and Impact*, Zoltan J. Acs, ed. (Boston: Kluwer Academic Publishers, 1999), p. 100.
[42] Joshua Lerner, "Small Business, Innovation, and Public Policy," in *Are Small Firms Important? Their Role and Impact,* p. 160.
[43] Ibid., p. 160.
[44] Bo Carlsson, "Small Business, Entrepreneurship, and Industrial Dynamics," p. 109.
[45] See Candida Brush and Robert D. Hisrich, "Women-Owned Businesses: Why Do They Matter?," in *Are Small Firms Important? Their Role and Impact*, pp. 111-127.
[46] See John Sibley Butler and Patricia Gene Greene, "Don't Call Me Small: The Contribution of Ethnic Enterprises to the Economic and Social Well-Being of America," in *Are Small Firms Important? Their Role and Impact* (Boston: Kluwer Academic Publishers, 1999), pp. 129-145.
[47] Douglas Holtz-Eakin and Harvey Rosen, *Economic Policy and the Start-up, Survival, and Growth of Entrepreneurial Ventures*, report submitted to the Small Business Administration, May 2001, pp. 43-44.
[48] For more information on market failures, see Joseph E. Stiglitz, *Economics of the Public Sector*, 3rd Edition (New York: W.W. Norton & Co., 2000), pp. 76-90.
[49] According to a 1990 study by Charles Brown, James Hamilton, and James Medoff, the average family owning a small business had an income that was 80% greater and wealth that was five times greater than the average family. (See Charles Brown, James Hamilton, and James

Medoff, *Employers Large and Small* (Cambridge, MA: Harvard University Press, 1990), pp. 15-17.) More recently, in a study of the wealth and income of U.S. small business owners from 1992 to 2001, researchers George W. Haynes and Charles Ou found that, in 2001, the mean income of households with small business owners was $110,370, compared to $42,108 for households with no business owners, and the mean net worth of households with small business owners was $1,050,872, compared to $188,535 for households with no business owners. (See George W. Haynes and Charles Ou, *How Did Small Business-Owning Households Fare During the longest U.S. Economic Expansion?*, report prepared for the Small Business Administration (Washington: June 2006) table 3, p. 26.

[50] Stiglitz, *Economics of the Public Sector*, pp. 567-569.

[51] Douglas Holtz-Eakin, "Should Small Businesses be Tax-Favored?," *National Tax Journal*, vol. 48, no. 3, Sept. 1995, p. 390.

[52] U.S. Small Business Administration, Office of Advocacy, *Frequently Asked Questions*, (Washington: Sept. 2008).

[53] See David Birch and James Medoff, "Gazelles," in *Labor Markets, Employment Policy, and Job Creation*, Lewis C. Solomon and Alec R. Levenson, eds. (Boulder, CO: Westview Press, 1994), p. 162. The share of net new jobs created by firms with 100 or fewer workers can exceed 100% in a year if these firms create more jobs than they destroy, all other firms destroy more jobs than they create, and the net job gain arising from the former exceeds the net job loss arising from the latter. For example, if firms with 100 or fewer employees account for a net job gain of 100 and all other firms generate a net job loss of 25, then the economy as a whole would realize a net job gain of 75, and the share of that gain attributable to firms with 100 or fewer employees would be 133%.

[54] Ibid., p. 8.

[55] Birch and Medoff, "Gazelles," pp. 162-164.

[56] Steven J. Davis, John C. Haltiwanger, and Scott Schuh, *Job Creation and Destruction* (Cambridge, MA: MIT Press, 1996), pp. 169-170.

[57] Scott J. Wallsten, "Rethinking the Small Business Innovation Research Program," in *Investing in Innovation: Creating a Research and Innovation Policy That Works*, Lewis M. Branscomb and James H. Keller, eds. (Cambridge, MA: MIT Press, 1998), p. 197.

[58] National Science Foundation, *U.S. Business R&D Expenditures Increase in 2006; Companies' Own and Federal Contributions Rise,* Info Brief (NSF-08-313), August 2008, table 1, p. 2.

[59] See Wallsten, "Rethinking the Small Business Innovation Research Program," p. 197.

[60] F. M. Scherer and David Ross, *Industrial Market Structure and Economic Performance*, 3rd edition (Boston: Houghton Mifflin Co., 1990), pp. 651-657.

[61] The estimate assumes a rate of inflation of 2% and a corporate tax rate of 35%. It is based on a simulation done by Gravelle with the aid of the CRS capital stock model on May 9, 2003.

[62] Holtz-Eakin, "Should Small Businesses Be Tax-Favored?" p. 393.

[63] Ibid.

# CHAPTER SOURCES

The following chapters have been previously published:

Chapter 1 – This is an edited, excerpted and augmented edition of a Small Business Administration, Office of Advocacy publication, Contract Number SBAHQ-07-Q-00Q12, dated April 2009.

Chapter 2 – This is an edited, excerpted and augmented edition of a United States Congressional Research Service publication, Report Order Code RL31852, dated March 18, 2009.

Chapter 3 – This is an edited, excerpted and augmented edition of a United States Congressional Research Service publication, Report Order Code RL32254, dated March 26, 2009.

# INDEX

## C



## D

## G



## H



## I



## J

K



L



M



N

## S



## T

## U



## V



## W



## Y